OVERNIGHT BOOK

PEOPLES AND CULTURES OF AFRICA

WEST AFRICA

Edited by Peter Mitchell

CHELSEA HOUSE
PUBLISHERS

An imprint of Infobase Publishing

Chelsea House
An imprint of Infobase Publishing
132 West 31st Street
New York, NY 10001

Library of Congress Cataloging-in-Publication Data

Peoples and cultures of Africa / edited by Peter Mitchell.
    p. cm.
    "Authors, Amy-Jane Beer ... [et al.]"—T.p. verso.
    Includes bibliographical references and index.

    Set ISBN 0-8160-6260-9 (acid-free paper)

Nations & Personalities of Africa ISBN 0-8160-6266-8
Peoples and Cultures of Southern Africa ISBN 0-8160-6265-X
Peoples and Cultures of Central Africa ISBN 0-8160-6264-1
Peoples and Cultures of East Africa ISBN 0-8160-6263-3
Peoples and Cultures of West Africa ISBN 0-8160-6262-5
Peoples and Cultures of North Africa ISBN 0-8160-6261-7

    1. Africa—Civilization. 2. Ethnology—Africa. I. Beer, Amy-Jane. II. Mitchell, Peter, 1962-
    DT14.P46 2006
    960—dc22

                                2006040011

Chelsea House books are available at special discounts when purchased in bulk quantities for businesses, associations, institutions, or sales promotions. Please call our Special Sales Department in New York at (212) 967-8800 or (800) 322-8755.

You can find Chelsea House on the World Wide Web at
http://www.chelseahouse.com

Printed and bound in China

10 9 8 7 6 5 4 3 2 1

For The Brown Reference Group plc.
Project Editor: Graham Bateman
Editors: Peter Lewis, Virginia Carter
Cartographers: Darren Awuah, Mark Walker
Designers: Steve McCurdy, Martin Anderson
Managing Editor: Bridget Giles
Production Director: Alastair Gourlay
Editorial Director: Lindsey Lowe

Consultant Editor

Dr. Peter Mitchell is University Lecturer in African Prehistory, and holds a Tutorial Fellowship in Archaeology at St. Hugh's College, University of Oxford, United Kingdom. He is also Curator of African Archaeology at the Pitt Rivers Museum, Oxford, and an academic member of the multidisciplinary African Studies Centre based at St. Antony's College, Oxford. He has previously worked at the University of Cape Town. He serves on the Governing Council of the British Institute in Eastern Africa and is a member of the editorial boards of numerous journals. From 2004–2006 he held the post of President of the Society of Africanist Archaeologists.

Advisory Editor

Dr. David Johnson is University Lecturer in Comparative and International Education (Developing Countries) and a Fellow of St. Antony's College, University of Oxford, United Kingdom. He is a member of the African Studies Centre, based at St. Antony's College, and has conducted research into education in a wide range of African countries. He serves on the United Kingdom National Commission for UNESCO's working committee on Africa and on the editorial boards of two international journals.

Authors

Anne Haour
with
Amy-Jane Beer
Amanda Berlan
Peter Mitchell
Ana-Margarida Santos

Title page *A Nigerian woman painting a mural on her house.*

CONTENTS

Peoples and Cultures of Africa provides a region-based study of Africa's main ethnic groups, cultures, languages, religions, music, and much more. Five of the six volumes cover large geographical regions, namely: **North Africa, West Africa, East Africa, Central Africa**, and **Southern Africa**. Each of these volumes starts with a series of overview articles covering the political situation today, physical geography, biomes, peoples, cultures, and finally a historical time line. The main articles that follow are arranged A–Z with four types of articles, each distinguished by a characteristic running-head logo and color panel:

ETHNIC GROUPS, such as Maasai, Zulu, Yoruba. Each ethnic group article includes a Fact File and a map, giving the approximate area in which a people mainly live.

MATERIAL CULTURE, such as Contemporary Art, Metalwork, Sculpture, Textiles

PERFORMING ARTS AND LITERATURE, such as African-language Literature, Masks and Masquerade, Dance and Song

RELIGION, SOCIETY, AND CULTURE, such as Islam, Christianity, Marriage and the Family

The sixth volume (**Nations and Personalities**) is divided into three main sections: *Political and Physical Africa* presents a complete overview of Africa, followed by profiles of every nation on the continent; *International Organizations* and *Environmental Organizations* review major international bodies operating in the region; and *African Personalities* gives biographies of some 300 people from throughout Africa.

Within each volume there is a *Glossary* of key terms, lists of *Further Resources* such as other reference books, and useful Web sites. Volume *Indexes* are provided in volumes 1–5, with a complete *Set Index* in volume 6.

WEST AFRICA TODAY

THE BORDERS OF THE 17 COUNTRIES THAT MAKE UP MODERN WEST AFRICA REFLECT DECISIONS THAT WERE TAKEN BY COLONIAL POWERS IN THE 19TH AND 20TH CENTURIES. CUTTING ACROSS ETHNIC AND CULTURAL DIVIDES, THESE FRONTIERS HAVE BEEN THE CAUSE OF MANY OF THE REGION'S MOST SERIOUS CONFLICTS. YET THIS DENSELY POPULATED AREA IS ALSO NOTED FOR ITS ECONOMIC DRIVE AND ENTREPRENEURIAL SPIRIT.

A political map of West Africa. With more than 128 million inhabitants, Nigeria is the most heavily populated country in Africa, and is the economic powerhouse of the region.

POVERTY AND CONFLICT

West Africa is one of the most underprivileged regions of the world, whether this is judged by the commonest yardstick—gross national product (GNP)—or by measures of human development such as life expectancy, education, food security, or access to clean water. Poorly developed communication networks and the great distances to be covered make the movement of both goods and people expensive.

This region has also been blighted by two recent conflicts: a long-running regional war involving Liberia, Sierra Leone, and Guinea (1990–2003), and a civil war in Côte d'Ivoire (2000–04). Even though the fighting has died down at time of writing, the situation in these countries remains of great concern, since insecurity continues to threaten the lives of ordinary citizens and limit economic performance.

Gulf of Guinea

A LAND OF OPPORTUNITIES

However, modern West Africa can also boast a number of success stories. It is a region of stock markets, mobile phones, Internet cafés, expanding transport networks, and a growing middle class. Fair and free elections are now a regular feature of the political landscape of many of the region's countries. The Ghana Stock Exchange regularly tops the list of the world's highest-performing markets. New internal airline companies are shrinking distances between the cities of this vast region.

One of the major trends throughout the region has been for increasing urbanization. In 2003 it was estimated that about 600,000 people were on the move each year, with almost half of them moving from rural to urban areas. The concentration of people along the coast is particularly noticeable. One out of five Nigerians, for example, lives along the coast, and the coastal city of Lagos and its immediate surroundings contain 85 percent of the country's industrial activity.

The crowded Oshodi market in the Nigerian city of Lagos. This open-air market is a hive of activity, where people sell a huge range of goods.

In Senegal, two-thirds of people are concentrated in the coastal region near Dakar, where 90 percent of the country's industries are situated.

The Economic Community of West African States (ECOWAS), created in 1975, includes all the West African states except Mauritania, which withdrew in 2000. This body promotes cooperation, economic growth, and integration. It entitles member countries to various duty exemptions, eased movement of peoples, and access to a joint peacekeeping force in times of crisis. The ECOWAS economies are at varying stages of development: Nigeria's economy stands out as the region's largest, exceeding that of all other ECOWAS countries combined. There is significant potential for an increase in Nigerian oil exports in years to come. However, oil exploration in Nigeria has long been associated with a cycle of violence and corruption and dispossession of Niger delta peoples (such as the Ogoni) on whose land oil reserves are located.

Most trade is conducted through the coastal ports of West Africa, and these are the areas where transport infrastructure is most highly developed.

The region's principal export commodities are energy products (crude oil, refined petroleum, and associated products), minerals (gold, diamonds, and bauxite) and agricultural goods (cocoa, coffee, groundnuts, and cotton).

A man and boy paddle their canoe past an oil jetty in the Niger Delta region of Nigeria. Oil drives the Nigerian economy, but the environmental and human cost of exploration is high.

PHYSICAL WEST AFRICA

WEST AFRICA IS BORDERED ON THE WEST AND SOUTH BY THE ATLANTIC OCEAN AND ON THE SOUTHEAST BY THE ADAMAWA HIGHLANDS OF CAMEROON. THE NORTHERN REGION ON THE FRINGE OF THE SAHARA IS KNOWN AS THE SAHEL, AND IS PRONE TO DROUGHT AND DESERT EXPANSION. THERE IS A NARROW, LOWLAND COASTAL STRIP BUT MOST OF WEST AFRICA COMPRISES PLATEAUS, WITH SOME MOUNTAINS TO THE NORTH AND SOUTH.

Map showing the main physical features of West Africa. The humid, fertile coastal regions are densely peopled, while the dry climate and poor soils of the north support only a shifting, seminomadic population.

West Africa occupies the Bulge of Africa, a great landmass projecting into the Atlantic Ocean. It encompasses a wide variety of environments, from rainforest in the far southeast of the region to the semiarid landscape of the Sahel in the north.

PLATEAUS AND COASTAL LOWLANDS

The plateaus that cover much of West Africa generally do not exceed 1,600 feet (500 m) in height and lack any major obstacles. Some of the higher such regions are the highlands of Guinea in the southwest, the Jos Plateau of Nigeria, and the Adamawa Highlands. The relative accessibility of the terrain fostered contacts between people from the earliest times, and West Africa became famous as a center of manufacture and trade.

The low-lying coast of West Africa is backed by a low plain. This area is the site of much agriculture and other economic activity, and is heavily populated.

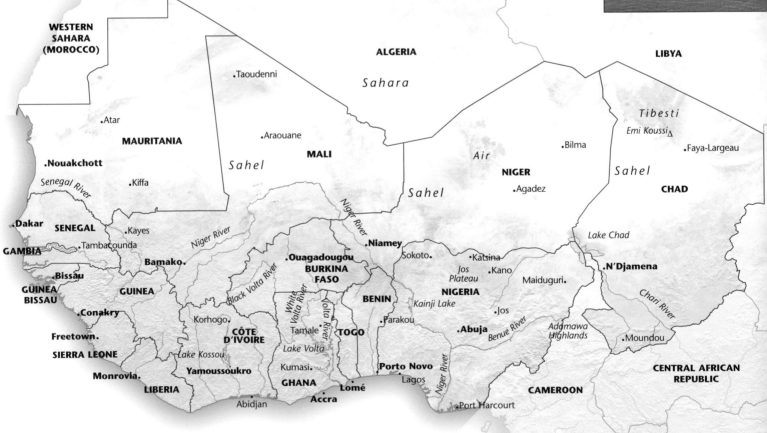

Gulf of Guinea

the Volta (Ghana and Burkina Faso), and the Benue in Nigeria. There are also countless seasonal rivers in the north that fill up after flash floods and provide a focus for settlement.

Lake Chad is a vitally important body of water. Its surface area varies greatly, since its water level fluctuates with rainfall and evaporation. It has also been steadily shrinking as a result of lower rainfall, overgrazing of the land, a growing population, and increased irrigation in the region. The lake covered 9,700 square miles (25,000 sq km) in 1963, but by 2001 had shrunk to just one-twentieth of that size. Another major body of water is the extensive Inner Delta of the Niger River in Mali. Lake Volta in Ghana, Lake Kossou in Côte d'Ivoire, and Kainji Lake in Nigeria are all large, artificial bodies of water created by the building of dams.

HIGHLANDS AND ISLANDS

West Africa's highest peaks are volcanoes. Emi Koussi, in the Tibesti mountains of northern Chad is the highest point, at 11,204 feet (3,415 m). Volcanic soils in the southwest, around the Jos plateau, have created some of the most fertile farmland in the region. Peaks over 6,000 feet (1,800 m) occur in Niger's Aïr mountains.

West Africa has a number of offshore islands such as the Cape Verde archipelago. Santo Antão on the Cape Verde islands is Africa's westernmost point.

RIVERS AND LAKES

The major geographical feature of West Africa is the Niger River. The modern nations of Niger and Nigeria, through whose territory it flows, are named for it. Running for over 2,500 miles (4,000 km), it is one of the world's longest rivers, but it also has one of the most unusual courses. Its source is just 150 miles (240 km) inland from the Atlantic, but it initially flows away from the sea, through Guinea and Mali, to water the fringes of the Sahara. It then takes a sharp right turn, known as the "Niger bend" to head back to the sea through Niger, Benin, and Nigeria. It is a vital natural resource for both farmers and seminomadic livestock herders in the Sahel. Other major rivers include the Senegal and the Gambia, both giving their name to the countries they flow through; the Casamance (southern Senegal),

Fishermen haul in their catch on the Niger River. The Niger, Africa's third-longest river, has both a coastal delta and an inland delta, which support much fishing, farming, and grazing.

LYING JUST NORTH OF THE EQUATOR, WEST AFRICA IS COMPLETELY WITHIN THE TROPICS. THE SOUTHERN COAST IS EXTREMELY WET—ONSHORE WINDS BLOWING IN FROM THE ATLANTIC OCEAN BRING HEAVY RAINFALL. IN CONTRAST, FARTHER NORTH, ON THE SOUTHERN FRINGES OF THE SAHARA, RAINFALL IS MINIMAL.

DESERT: THE SAHARA

The southern edge of the Sahara, the world's largest desert, extends into northern areas of Mauritania, Mali, Niger, and Chad. Relatively small areas of the desert constitute the "classic" desert landscape of towering sand dunes. Much of the rest is rocky plateaus (*hammadas*), and well over half is flat plain covered in thin, dry soil known as yermosol, lying over beds of gravel. The region experiences little or no rainfall in the course of a year, and there is virtually no surface water. This has not always been

1

4

Animal species of West Africa: 1 *Vervet monkey* (Chlorocebus aethiops); 2 *Leopard* (Panthera pardus); 3 *Western gorilla* (Gorilla gorilla); 4 *Royal python* (Python regius); 5 *Common chimpanzee* (Pan troglodytes); 6 *African porcupine* (Hystrix cristata).

Deserts and xeric shrublands
Tropical and subtropical grasslands, savannas, and shrubland
Tropical and subtropical moist broadleaf forests
Flooded grasslands
Water

WESTERN SAHARA (MOROCCO)

ALGERIA

LIBYA

.Taoudenni

Sahara

.Atar

Tibesti

Emi Koussi △

.Araouane

.Bilma

.Faya-Largeau

MAURITANIA

MALI

Air

.Nouakchott

Sahel

Sahel

NIGER

Sahel

.Kiffa

Sahel

.Agadez

CHAD

Senegal River

.Dakar SENEGAL

.Kayes

Niger River

.Niamey

Sokoto.

.Katsina

Lake Chad

GAMBIA

Tambacounda

Niger River

.Kano

.N'Djamena

.Bissau

Bamako.

.Ouagadougou

BURKINA FASO

Jos Plateau

Maiduguri.

GUINEA BISSAU

GUINEA

Black Volta River

BENIN

NIGERIA

.Conakry

Korhogo.

White Volta River

Volta River

Parakou.

Kainji Lake

.Jos

Chari River

Freetown.

CÔTE D'IVOIRE

Tamale.

TOGO

.Abuja

Benue River

Adamawa Highlands

.Moundou

SIERRA LEONE

Lake Volta

Kumasi.

Porto Novo

Niger River

CENTRAL AFRICAN REPUBLIC

Monrovia.

Yamoussoukro

GHANA

Lomé.

Lagos.

LIBERIA

Abidjan.

Accra.

CAMEROON

.Port Harcourt

Gulf of Guinea

woodland dominated by acacia and tamarind trees, with jujube and baobab in slightly wetter areas. Much of the land is given over to pasture or arable farming—sorghum, millet, and cotton are grown for subsistence and as cash crops. Characteristic wildlife include baboons and patas monkeys and striped and spotted hyenas.

TROPICAL MOIST BROADLEAF FOREST: COASTAL FOREST

The broad strip of land along West Africa's southern coast receives up to 47 inches (1,200 mm) of rain annually. In undeveloped areas, the land is covered by an extension of the dense tropical rainforests that dominate the Congo Basin in Central Africa. The forest is broken up by zones of mangroves and freshwater swamp, and patches of grassland and wooded savanna. This kind of mosaic habitat brings high biodiversity, including some of the world's most important populations of gorilla, mandrill, and chimpanzee. However, much of the region's wildlife is under threat from human expansion, hunting, and war. The pygmy hippopotamus is found exclusively in this region, along with several monkeys and 13 species of amphibians. More than half of the region's c.8,000 plant species are thought to grow nowhere else on Earth.

the case—evidence from rock art and fossils and other remains suggest than the area was home to hippopotamuses, elephants, and crocodiles as recently as 6,000 years ago. Today only species adapted to extremely dry conditions can survive here—for example dorcas gazelles, Egyptian plovers, and fennec (desert) foxes. Vegetation is limited mainly to the moister valleys (wadis) and oases. Acacia and tamarind trees grow in these areas, while the *hammadas* may support hardy herbs such as antirrhinum.

TROPICAL GRASSLAND/SAVANNA: THE SAHEL

The word *Sahel* comes from the Arabic for "shore," and refers to the region's location on the edge of the great sea of sand that is the Sahara. Sadly, the Sahel is suffering from increasing desertification. This process occurs when drought, a sudden influx of people (through forced resettlement), and overgrazing by livestock erode the topsoil of a semidesert region and denude it of vegetation. Desertification forces people and animals to migrate in search of food and water. The rains are more reliable in the south of the region, which is dominated by vast tracts of dry grassland and scrubby

Lush tropical rainforest covers much of the Volta region of southern Ghana and supports a great variety of wildlife.

WEST AFRICA IS CHARACTERIZED BY ITS EXTREME ETHNIC AND LINGUISTIC DIVERSITY. COMMUNITIES ARE AT THE SAME TIME VERY DISTINCT FROM ONE ANOTHER IN LANGUAGE, DRESS, AND CUSTOMS, BUT ALSO IN CONSTANT INTERACTION WITH EACH OTHER.

RELIGION

There are three main forms of religion in West Africa: Islam, Christianity, and indigenous African religions. The latter term embraces many different faiths, but generally speaking they share a belief in the existence of individual spirits inhabiting natural objects. A tree, mountain, or stone may be sacred because it represents a spirit. All West Africans once followed this form of religion, until trans-Saharan traders spread Islam and missionaries brought Christianity. Many

Below and opposite: Summary family trees of the Nilo-Saharan, Afro-Asiatic, and Niger-Congo language groups. The ethnic groups featured in this volume are listed in parentheses after the relevant language.

Map showing the distribution of the population in West Africa. The people of this densely populated region live predominantly on the coast and in the fertile river valleys.

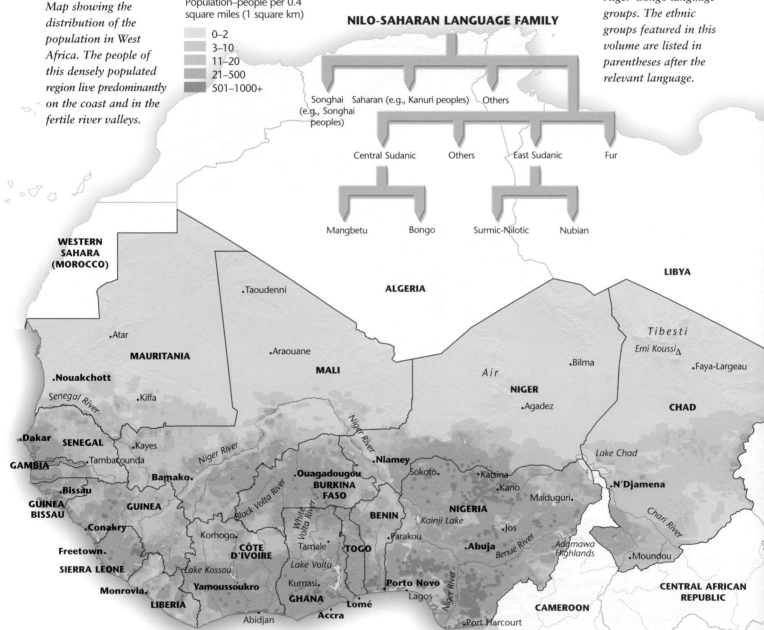

Population–people per 0.4 square miles (1 square km)

- 0–2
- 3–10
- 11–20
- 21–500
- 501–1000+

NILO-SAHARAN LANGUAGE FAMILY

Songhai (e.g., Songhai peoples) — Saharan (e.g., Kanuri peoples) — Others

Central Sudanic — Others — East Sudanic — Fur

Mangbetu — Bongo — Surmic-Nilotic — Nubian

AFRO-ASIATIC LANGUAGE FAMILY

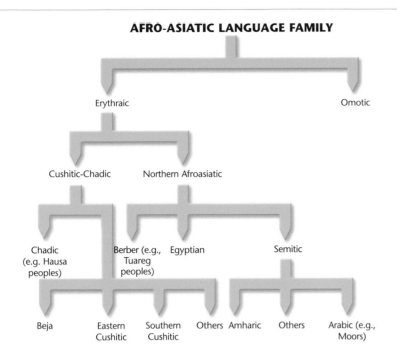

people today still practice African religions. For example, half of the population of Togo follow preexisting belief systems. There is also a high degree of mixing, with many people observing some aspects of preexisting faiths alongside Christian or Muslim observance.

While preexisting religious practices were based on oral history traditions, Islam and Christianity rely on written scriptures. Islam was introduced to West Africa from about 750 C.E. onward, principally by Muslim Berber and Arab traders from North Africa. Christianity arrived mainly via European merchants on the West African coast from about 1450. However, people did not convert in substantial numbers until the mid-19th century. Generally speaking, Christianity is today more widespread on the coast—in a country like Ghana, almost two-thirds of people are Christian—while Islam is common in the Sahel (the area immediately to the south of the Sahara). In Mali, for example, 90 percent of the population is Muslim.

LANGUAGES

West African languages are extremely diverse. More than 400 languages are currently spoken in Nigeria alone, for example. Languages from no fewer than three different language families are spoken in West Africa: Afro-Asiatic, Nilo-Saharan, and Niger-Congo.

Several non-African languages are also spoken. French is the official language of half of West Africa. English is the second most common, being the official language of five countries—Gambia, Ghana, Liberia, Nigeria, and Sierra Leone. Portuguese is the official language of Cape Verde and Guinea-Bissau, and Arabic that of Mauritania.

A number of linguae francae—convenient common trade languages—are also used in West Africa. Such languages developed and spread along commercial routes: they include Fula (the language of the Fulani), Hausa, and Arabic. Many West Africans speak several languages; it is not uncommon to meet someone who speaks Hausa at home, Zarma with friends, French at work, a little Arabic at the mosque, and some English.

NIGER-CONGO LANGUAGE FAMILY

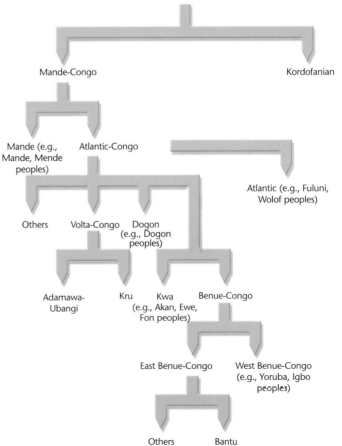

WEST AFRICA IS DESERVEDLY FAMOUS FOR THE GREAT DIVERSITY OF ITS CULTURAL AND ARTISTIC TRADITIONS. FROM THE BEAUTIFUL SCULPTURES OF NOK, IFE, AND BENIN TO THE VERVE OF MODERN WEST AFRICAN MUSIC, ART AND CULTURE FROM THIS REGION HAVE MADE A DEEP AND LASTING IMPRESSION ON THE OUTSIDE WORLD.

MATERIAL ARTS: SCULPTURE, MASKS, AND TEXTILES

Archaeological finds of 2,500-year-old clay statuettes produced by the Nok Culture indicate that skilled craftspeople were working in West Africa from ancient times. Sophisticated metal casting using the lost-wax technique (which involves first making a mold of the object to be cast in clay and wax, resulting in intricate and lifelike detail) was employed as early as the Igbo-Ukwu culture of Nigeria, around 1,200 years ago.

Under colonialism, the seizure of art works by foreign powers (such as the "bronzes" of the kingdom of Benin) saw many ancient artifacts taken to collections and galleries outside Africa. Illegal exports in the postcolonial period further depleted West Africa's heritage.

Masks are an evocative and well-known aspect of West African culture. Made of wood, metal, leather, cloth, glass beads, or fibers, they come in a huge range of sizes and shapes: from the Dan "passport masks" (carried as a protective charm) of Liberia and Côte d'Ivoire, which are only 3–4 inches (8–10 cm) high, to the tall Dogon masks of Mali. Most are worn during dances, accompanied by music and signing, to mark important social events and honor the gods or, increasingly, to celebrate and entertain.

Textiles, whether produced locally or imported from European markets, are a vibrant and ever-present feature of the West African street scene. West Africa is noted for its colorful printed cloth; the ceremonial kente worn by the Asante of Ghana is known worldwide. Women are important consumers of African textiles; a typical outfit involves three separate lengths of cloth, making up a shirt, a skirt, and an outside wrap worn around the waist or the head. The indigo-dyed cotton cloth produced by the nomadic Tuareg has given them their popular name "blue men of the desert"; the

KRU

The Kru people mainly live in southern Liberia and southwestern Côte d'Ivoire. Their name is thought to come from the English word *crew*, since Kru speakers have long been known for working on ships on Africa's western seaboard. Historically, the Kru lived by fishing or farming. The civil wars in Liberia and Côte d'Ivoire around the turn of the 21st century have brought great upheaval and change. Many people have been displaced, and more Kru groups now live outside their traditional areas than within them. The contender for the Liberian presidency in 2005 and former international soccer star George Weah (b.1966) comes from a Kru family.

The Kru were among the earliest West African converts to Christianity. William Wadé Harris (c.1865–1929), a Grebo (a Kru subgroup), founded an evangelical movement called the Harrist Church in the 19th century that converted more than 120,000 people.

Kru sailors invented the musical style known as Highlife that became widely popular throughout Africa in the 1950s and 1960s. Kru musicians imported this blend of jazz, swing, and Cuban music plus a homegrown guitar sound to Ghana, where it took firm root.

dye in this fabric rubs off onto wearer's skin, giving it a bluish tinge. Decorative cloths such as *bogolan* from Mali (also called mud cloth as mud is used in its manufacture) and Fulani woven mats are extremely popular for making wall coverings and bedcovers.

WEST AFRICAN MUSIC

West Africa has long had a culture of oral history and performance by special castes of storytellers called *jali* or griots. This tradition has contributed to the rise of an incredibly rich modern music scene in West Africa. The fame of many performers has spread worldwide, such as the Malian guitarist Ali Farka Touré (1949–2006) and his compatriot, the singer Salif Keita (b.1949). In Senegal, the Tukulor singer Baaba Maal (b.1954) is renowned for his strong, clear voice), while the bustling capital and port of Dakar is home to the lively sound of Youssou N'Dour (b.1959) and the influential guitar-based band Orchestra Baobab.

Maskers of the Senufo Poro society. The kponiugo *helmet mask (foreground) represents a mythical being who protects the community from sorcerers. Masks are a key part of many West African rituals.*

1,000,000–60,000 years ago Hand-axes indicate human presence in West Africa.

70,000–12,000 years ago Evidence of stone tool manufacture demonstrates that all parts of West Africa are inhabited by this time.

9,500 years ago Pottery with a variety of shapes and impressed decorations is being produced in several parts of the Sahara and Sahel.

5,000 years ago Hunter-gatherer and cattle-herding societies exist throughout West Africa.

4,000–3,000 years ago Nomadic hunter-gatherer existence gives way to settled agriculture in both Sahel and forest, e.g., at Dhar Tichit in what is now Mauritania; millet cultivation begins; in present-day Ghana, people of the Kintampo culture manufacture pottery and make stone tools.

4,000–2,500 years ago Hierarchical societies (based on rank) begin to develop in West Africa.

3,000–2,000 years ago Copper and iron are first used in many areas throughout West Africa.

2,500 years ago Taruga, Nigeria, becomes a major center of ironworking.

2,500 years ago The elaborate Nok culture, with its tradition of terracotta sculpture, flourishes in what is now Nigeria.

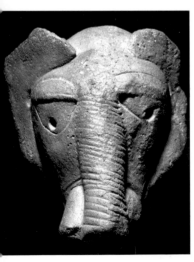

A terracotta elephant's head from the Iron Age Nok Culture, which existed in what is now Nigeria from 2,500 years ago to 200 C.E.

2,500 years ago–800 years ago People settle on high ground at Jenné-jeno and Dia-Shoma along the Niger River in what is now Mali; first town in sub-Saharan Africa develops at Jenné-jeno and becomes a walled city by c.400 C.E.

8th–11th centuries C.E. The Za dynasty rules the Songhai state, from Kukiya and later from Gao in eastern Mali, building trans-Saharan trade contacts; clans of the Soninke people come together to create the kingdom of Ghana around Kumbi Saleh in present-day Mauritania.

9th century Bronze ceremonial objects made for the first time at Igbo-Ukwo (Nigeria); thousands of imported beads found at this site indicate the presence of a well-structured society with wide-ranging trade contacts.

9th–10th centuries Islam becomes established among many communities in the Sahel and Sahara, for example at Aïr (Niger); rulers of Songhai and Kanem-Borno convert around this time.

9th–12th centuries Yoruba city-state of Ife in southwestern Nigeria, established in the sixth century, is the dominant regional power.

999 Kano, one of the seven Hausa city-states, is founded in Nigeria, according to the ancient *Kano Chronicle*.

1076 The Almoravid emirate—founded by the Sanhaja Berber leader Yahya ibn Masa—and based in Morocco and western Algeria—strengthens West Africa's links with the Muslim world.

1200–1700 Centers of Islamic learning flourish in cities such as Anisaman (Niger), Timbuktu (ancient Mali), and Kano (Nigeria), with libraries and visits from scholars from throughout the Muslim world.

c.1210 Dunama Dibalami becomes ruler of Kanem-Borno, leading it to the height of its power.

c.1230 The Mali empire grows around the upper Niger inland delta under the leadership of Sundiata Keita.

c.1250 Center of Yoruba power shifts from Ife northwest to Oyo; the Edo people establish the Kingdom of Benin in modern southwesterrn Nigeria.

c.1260–70 Mansa Uli, son of Sundiata, expands the Mali empire, and is first Mali leader to go on pilgrimage (hajj) to Mecca.

1324–25 Mansa Musa, ruler of Mali 1307–32, goes on the hajj with 8,000 men and two tons of gold, establishing Mali's reputation as a major power.

1380s According to the *Kano Chronicle*, the Wangara arrive in the Hausa town of Kano and Muslim prayer is held throughout the land.

c.1400 Building on centuries of tradition, the kingdoms of Benin and Ife become major centers of metal casting, producing objects for royal courts and shrines.

1432 Portuguese navigators begin exploring the West African coast.

1455 In one of the first European accounts of West Africa, Venetian sailor Alviso Ca da Mosto describes the Kayor kingdom of the Wolof and the salt and gold trade of Mali.

1464–92 Sonni Ali Ber frees Songhai lands from rule by Mali empire and establishes the Songhai empire.

The powerful Kingdom of Benin, founded by the Edo people of southern Nigeria, traded extensively with the Portuguese and Dutch from the 1400s onward. It was renowned for its craft guilds, foremost among which were those of the metalworkers. This brass plaque shows an oba *(king) flanked by attendants.*

1471–82 After venturing down the West African coast, the Portuguese found the fort of São Jorge da Mina (Elmina, in what is now Ghana), the earliest known European structure in the tropics. At this thriving trade center, cloth, beads, brass, bracelets, and other goods are exchanged for gold and ivory (and later slaves, who are shipped across the Atlantic from here).

1472 The Portuguese colonize the Cape Verde Islands to create a base for trade with states on the African mainland.

1493 Askia Muhammad I seizes power in Songhai; he extends the empire to cover most of modern Chad, Niger, and Mali; under his rule Islamic scholarship flourishes in Timbuktu (modern Tombouctou).

Late 15th century The Hausa are mentioned for the first time by an outside (Egyptian) source; they trade extensively and compete with neighboring Kanem-Borno, Songhai, and Aïr. Weak rulers and escalating raids by Mossi neighbors and Tuareg Berbers gradually reduce the power of Mali; by 1500 it is eclipsed by Songhai.

c.1500 A number of independent Mossi states arise around the headwaters of the Volta river.

1517 A regular trade in slaves is instituted by the Spanish from the west coast of Africa to the Caribbean.

c.1520 Kingdom of Benin resists attempts to convert the state to Christianity, and expels Portuguese traders and missionaries.

1575 Idris III Aloma makes Kanem-Borno the most powerful state between the Niger and the Nile.

1591 The Songhai state, seriously weakened by internal strife, collapses after a Moroccan invasion.

17th century Three forest kingdoms develop among the Akan people: Akwamu, Akyem, and Denkyera; Denkyera becomes the most powerful, but is eclipsed by the breakaway Asante state by the 1670s.

1600–1800 European traders (mainly Portuguese, Dutch, British and French) grow rich on the profits of the transatlantic slave trade from the west coast of Africa. African kings (e.g. of Oyo) and merchants supply slaves in return for beads, textiles, liquor, horses, and guns. Sahel states are weakened by the rise of the coastal regions.

An early print of the fort at São Jorge da Mina, founded by the Portuguese in 1482. The settlement became a major center for the export of gold; Europeans named this area the Gold Coast. Another lucrative trade was in slaves; in total, some 12 million Africans were enslaved and shipped to the Americas.

1617–42 Dutch West India Company enters the West African slave trade, gaining control of the base at Gorée Island (Senegal) and conquering all former Portuguese forts along the Gold Coast.

1659–77 The French establish their presence in West Africa, building a fort at St Louis at the mouth of the Senegal river and capturing Gorée Island from the Dutch.

1660–1750 Several chronicles composed in Gao and Timbuktu at this time recount the history of the Sahel: the *Tarikh el-Fettach* describes the Songhai and their impact of adjoining nations, while the *Tedzkiret-en-Nisiân* records the Moroccan occupation of Timbuktu.

1660s The Bambara (Bamana) kingdoms of Kaarta and Ségou begin to estabish themselves as major slave-trading states on the upper Niger River.

1670–1701 The Asante empire rises to prominence under the leadership of Osei Tutu; based around Kumasi (modern Ghana), it becomes active in the slave trade.

1672 The Royal African Company is founded and granted a monopoly over the British slave trade in West Africa; it trades from Gambia to the mouth of the Niger River.

In 1787 Freetown (Sierra Leone) was chosen by British antislavery campaigners as the site of a colony for freed slaves. Tension soon arose between the settlers and local Temne people.

1720s Islamic state of Fouta Djallon (in modern Guinea) is founded by the Fulani; it is overrun by French forces in 1896.

1726–48 Series of wars along the Slave Coast between Oyo and Dahomey; the Oyo slave-trading state overcomes Dahomey and forces it to take part in slavery.

1758–83 British and French clash over control of coastal Senegal. France asserts rule over the area by 1817.

1780s The transatlantic slave trade is at its peak, with some 70,000 slaves being shipped to the Americas, including the Caribbean, each year; Britain is the leading nation in this trade at this time.

1787 Philanthropists establish Freetown in Sierra Leone as a colony for 400 freed slaves.

1804–09 Fulani leader Usman Dan Fodio leads a war of Islamic revolution and conversion (jihad) against the Hausa states and founds an important empire, the Sokoto caliphate (Nigeria).

A copper cent coin struck by the American Colonization Society for use in Liberia, the colony it founded in 1821. In 1847 Liberia became the first independent republic on the continent.

1807   British parliament declares the slave trade illegal throughout the British Empire.

1819–21 Sekou Amadou conducts a jihad to found the Macina empire around Hamdallahi in Mali.

1821–22 Liberia is established by the American Colonization Society as a colony for resettlement of former U.S. slaves.

1823–1902 Series of four wars (1823, 1826, 1863, and 1874) between the Asante and British forces finally sees the Asante empire annexed by Britain in 1902.

1828   French explorer René-Auguste Caillié is the first European to reach the town of Timbuktu in the Sahel.

1829–41 Ibadan empire emerges in Nigeria as a regional successor state to Oyo; it is conquered by the British in 1897.

1854–62 Umar Tal, leader of the Tukulor (settled Fulani), aiming to halt the progress of French colonization, conquers Macina (Mali) and establishes the short-lived Tukulor caliphate, which is overrun by French forces in 1892–97.

1868–80 Muslim leader Samori Touré founds a powerful chiefdom in Kankan region of Guinea, expanding it to extend from Upper Volta region to Fouta Djallon.

1881–98 Mande peoples revolt against French colonization, led by Samori Touré.

1884–85 The Berlin Conference on Africa agrees spheres of influence for the European colonization of Africa; by the late 1880s, the "Scramble for Africa," is in full swing, with West Africa divided between French, German, British, and Portuguese interests.

1893–1900 Sudanese Arab slave trader Rabeh bin Fadl Allah conquers Bornu and Bagirmi and creates a kingdom south of Lake Chad; it is later conquered by France.

1897   British forces overrun the Kingdom of Benin.

In the 19th century, European explorers vied with one another to reach the remote Malian city of Timbuktu—long a center of trans Saharan trade and Islamic learning. They were driven by false rumors of a city roofed with gold and bursting with riches.

1900–50 Raw materials and cash crops such as peanuts, cotton, coffee, cocoa, and rubber are produced cheaply in the West African colonies for the European markets.

1903 After more than 40 years of fighting (since 1861), the Sokoto caliphate is defeated and incorporated into the British colony of Nigeria.

1904 France creates a federation (French West Africa) covering the western part of its African empire, and based in Dakar (Senegal).

1914–18 Thousands of West Africans are drafted by the colonial powers to serve in World War I. Most fight in Africa, but France trains Senegalese troops as riflemen to serve in Europe.

1920s Strikes break out against colonial authorities in Sierra Leone, Gold Coast, and Nigeria as nationalist movements grow.

President Kwame Nkrumah salutes the crowd in Accra as the former British colony of the Gold Coast gains independence as the republic of Ghana on March 6, 1957.

1922 Togoland, Germany's only West African territory, is divided between Britain and France after Germany's defeat in World War I.

1930s In Paris, French-speaking West Africans and others found the negritude literary movement, promoting black self-awareness and pride.

1935 Almost 40 years after the last Asante ruler Prempeh I was deposed by the British, the Asante monarchy is restored in the Gold Coast colony.

1939–45 West African troops fight on the Allied side in World War II; the Gold Coast (Ghanaian) ports of Accra, Tema, and Takoradi become vital staging posts for ferrying war materials to Allied armies fighting the Germans in North Africa.

1945–65 A rising tide of nationalism, led by charismatic figures such as Kwame Nkrumah of Ghana, Felix Houphouët-Boigny of Côte d'Ivoire, and Djibo Bakari of Niger, results in the independence of almost all West African nations by 1965.

1945 A common currency (CFA franc) is launched to serve the French-speaking countries of the Union Economique et Monétaire Ouest Africaine (UEMOA): Benin, Burkina Faso, Côte d'Ivoire, Guinea-Bissau, Mali, Niger, Senegal, and Togo.

1957 The Gold Coast becomes the first African colony to gain independence, as Ghana.

1958–60 French colonies hold referendums on independence; after first resisting, France grants its colonies independence within the French Union in 1960.

Biafran soldiers man a machine-gun during the devastating civil war in Nigeria (1967–70). This conflict erupted when the Igbo tried to form a breakaway state.

1963 The Organization for African Unity (OAU) is formed. Military coups are staged in Dahomey and Togo.

1967–70 The Igbo break away from Nigeria and found the independent state of Biafra. In the civil war and famine that follow, more than 1 million people die.

1974–75 Guinea Bissau and the Cape Verde Islands achieve independence from Portugal. There are now 16 sovereign nations in West Africa.

1975 The Economic Community of West African States (ECOWAS) founded, with all the West African states as members (Mauritania later withdraws).

1977 Nigeria hosts an international Black Festival of the Arts.

1979 Flight-Lieutenant Jerry Rawlings stages a coup in Ghana (and again in 1981). Rawlings rules until 2000.

1980 A coup led by Master-Sergeant Samuel Doe ends over a century of continuous rule in Liberia by Americo-Liberians, who make up just 3 percent of the people.

1982 Senegal and Gambia unite to form the Senegambia Confederation, which is dissolved seven years later.

1986 Nigerian writer Wole Soyinka is awarded the Nobel Prize for Literature.

1987–89 Construction of the Basilica of Our Lady of Peace at Yamoussoukro in Côte d'Ivoire, the largest church in the world.

1989–2003 Liberia experiences two long-running civil wars that leave the country ruined and impoverished.

1990 First multiparty elections are held in Côte d'Ivoire as Felix Houphouët-Boigny, leader since independence in 1960, steps down.

1990–94 Tuareg, forced to migrate northward by severe droughts in the mid-1980s, come into conflict with Mali and Niger governments and stage uprisings in both countries.

1991–2000 Liberian civil war spills over into neighboring Sierra Leone.

1994 The CFA franc is devalued by 50 percent; hardships, strikes, and protests are widespread in CFA countries.

1995 Military government in Nigeria executes nine Ogoni activists, including the writer Ken Saro-Wiwa; Nigeria's membership of the Commonwealth is suspended.

1996 Kofi Annan of Ghana is elected as the seventh Secretary-General of the United Nations.

1999 The CFA franc is linked to the euro at the rate of 1 euro = 655,957 CFA.

2000–02 Violence erupts between Yoruba Christians and Hausa Muslims in Nigeria, following the introduction by six northern states of strict Islamic law (Sharia). Christian–Muslim rioting also forces the relocation of the "Miss World" pageant from Nigeria to London.

2001 The Organization for African Unity (OAU) is replaced by the African Union (AU); its aims are a common African currency, economic system, and foreign policy.

2002 More than 20 years after the official abolition of slavery in Mauritania, Amnesty International reports that it is still being practiced by the country's Arabs and Berbers.

2002–04 Fighting between rival rebel armies kills many thousands in Côte d'Ivoire; after growing antiforeigner attacks France intervenes to aid its expatriates.

2004–05 A widespread drought and crop failure brings famine to central Niger.

2005 The G8 group of the world's richest countries agree to cancel all debts owed by 18 developing countries, including seven West African nations: Benin, Burkina Faso, Ghana, Mali, Mauritania, Niger, and Senegal.

Refugees flee the civil war raging in Liberia in 1990. This conflict, which saw President Samuel Doe deposed and killed, lasted for six years, during which 150,000 people lost their lives.

PEOPLE PRACTICING AFRICAN RELIGIONS

Benin	50%	Liberia	40%
Burkina Faso	40%	Mali	9%
Cape Verde	1%	Mauritania	0%
Chad	7%	Niger	up to 20%
Côte d'Ivoire	25–40%	Nigeria	10%
Gambia	1%	Senegal	1%
Ghana	21%	Sierra Leone	30%
Guinea	7%	Togo	51%
Guinea-Bissau	50%		

The Igbo religion flourishes alongside Christianity in southeastern Nigeria. In addition to the benevolent creator-god Chukwu, there are many lesser deity-spirits called alusi. *It is the role of Igbo shamans such as the one shown above (at a ritual in Onitsha) to interpret the wishes of the alusi.*

THE FOLLOWERS OF AFRICAN RELIGIONS TEND TO BELIEVE IN A SINGLE CREATOR-GOD, WHO IS ASSISTED BY A LARGE NUMBER OF SPIRITS. ASSOCIATED WITH THE VARIOUS SPIRITS ARE SACRED SITES, WHERE RITUALS ARE HELD WITH SEPARATE ROLES RESERVED FOR MEN AND WOMEN.

West African religions are by no means extinct or a thing of the past. One of the largest groups of people in the region is the Yoruba. Before European colonialism, there existed several powerful Yoruba groups, whose rulers and people shared a complex belief system characterized by a huge number of deities. Common religious rituals and forms of organization helped bind the Yoruba together, giving them the unity of a nation-state.

Today, the Yoruba are fully integrated into the technological, industrial society of modern Nigeria. They retain a keen sense of their Yoruba identity, as expressed through their religion. Accordingly, in this community there is a strong and widespread allegiance to the Yoruba belief system, even among practicing Christians and Muslims. In some instances, where colonialism and missionary education had once caused many people to turn away from the Yoruba religion, there has recently been a strong revival of the traditional ways. In Oshogbo, for example (see FESTIVAL AND CEREMONY), shrines to an important Yoruba spirit-deity have been restored to form the centerpiece of a major annual festival.

Veneration of ancestors forms a key part of many of the religions of West Africa. Ancestral spirits are thought to watch over and influence the affairs of living people. Much attention is paid to ensuring that these spirits are given due respect, so that they will take care of the community. Rituals held in their honor are linked to key events such as births, deaths, marriages, and harvests, and are usually accompanied by music and dancing.

CROSS-CURRENTS

Islam had begun to establish itself in West Africa by around 1000 C.E., while Christianity was brought by European traders, slavers, and missionaries from the late 15th century onward. Among some peoples, such as the Moors, the Fulani, and the Hausa, the introduction of these world religions resulted in the decline of indigenous beliefs. By contrast, other cultures, notably those of the Fon of Benin and the Mende of Sierra Leone, resisted outside influence. Most commonly, however, a far less clear-cut situation emerged. West African Muslim and Christian converts incorporated many elements of their preexisting beliefs into their new faith, or continued to practice African rituals as well as those of the adopted religion. This remains the case in many cultures today.

Because the West African coast was the place from which most slaves were transported to the Americas, elements of the many religions of this region found their way into belief systems that developed among the people of the African diaspora in the New World. Vodun, now practiced in Haiti (which originated among the Fon), Candomblè (in Brazil), and Shango (in Trinidad, Grenada, and Brazil) are instances of such religions. These faiths blend together aspects from a number of religions. Santería, which is practiced on Cuba and other

A Yoruba shrine carving depicting the orisha *(spirit-deity) Oko. This male deity is associated with agriculture and the fertility of the land and is the patron spirit of farm workers. He is shown holding a cockerel and surrounded by many children, whom he provides for in his bounty.*

Caribbean islands, arose when Yoruba slaves shipped across the Atlantic by the Spanish began to mix their existing beliefs in a large number of Yoruba deities called the *orisha* (or *orisa*) with the cult of the saints in their masters' Roman Catholicism. (The slaves were forcibly converted to Catholicism on their arrival.) The most important *orisha* Obatala, who is the chief representative on Earth of the Yoruba creator-god Olodumare, came to be identified with the resurrected Jesus Christ. Likewise, the Catholic St. Barbara, who is associated with fire, lightning, and thunder, was equated with the storm-spirit Shango. *Santería* was originally a negative term (meaning "excessive veneration of saints") that the Spanish applied to their slaves' new faith, but which its followers later adopted themselves.

SEE ALSO: *Festival and ceremony; Mande; Masks and masquerade; Yoruba.*

WARDING OFF EVIL SPIRITS

The Serer of Senegal once believed in the existence of an unfriendly spirit-sorceress who withheld water from the arid lands in their region. Before Islam became widely established among the Serer, specialist diviners were called in to discover and appease the spirit who was responsible for delaying the rain.

Among the Mande, one of the tasks of the community's spiritual guide—who is known as the *kankouran*—is to protect orchards from harm by attaching fibers of his costume to the fruit trees. He also acts as the guardian of circumcised people.

The use of good-luck charms called *gri-gri* is widespread throughout West Africa. Fishers, for example, place lucky charms on their boats to guard against being drowned and to ensure a large catch. The charms often incorporate Arabic inscriptions from the Quran.

MAJOR WORKS AND THEIR AUTHORS

Title	Date	Author	Language
Bayan Wajub-al-Hijra ala'l-ibad	1806	Shaykh Usman dan Fodio	Hausa
Zuwan Nasara (Arrival of the Christians)	1903	Alhaji Umaru	Hausa
Iwe Ekini Sobo (Sobo's First Book)	1905	Sobowole Sowande	Yoruba
Sègilolá eléyinyú egé (Segilola of the Seductive Eyes)	1929	Isaac Babalola Thomas	Yoruba
Omenuko	1933	Pita Nwana	Igbo
Ogboju Ode Ninu Igbo Irunmale (Forest of One Thousand Demons)	1938	Daniel Olurunfemi Fagunwa	Yoruba
Oba Koso (The King Did Not Hang)	1963	Duro Ladipo	Yoruba
Ayanmo (Predestination)	1973	Afolabi Olabimtan	Yoruba
Aawo Bi	1990	Mame Younousse Dieng	Wolof

An ancient text from one of the Quranic libraries in Chinguetti, Mauritania. Islam was introduced to West Africa by trans-Saharan Berber traders in around 1000; one of the innovations the new faith brought was the written word.

WEST AFRICA HAS A TRADITION OF ORAL STORYTELLING RATHER THAN A LONG HISTORY OF WRITTEN LITERATURE, YET THE 20TH CENTURY WITNESSED THE RISE OF A DIVERSE LITERATURE DEALING WITH BOTH TIMELESS AND TOPICAL THEMES.

BEGINNINGS AND TRENDS

Written Arabic was used by Islamic scholars in the Sahel from around 1000 C.E. The first indigenous language to be written down was Hausa, in the early 1800s, using either the Arabic or the Roman alphabet. Notable early works in Hausa were those of the philosopher and revolutionary Usman dan Fodio (1754–1817). Yet most African languages did not have a written form until later in the 19th century, when European missionaries arrived in Africa and began translating the Bible.

Literature in African languages is very uncommon in former French colonies. There, writing in African languages was discouraged by the colonial authorities, who adopted a policy of cultural assimilation of the people they governed. Accordingly, French was strongly promoted as the official language. In general, the languages in which most African-language literature is published are those with the most speakers. Thus, West African-language literature is dominated by Yoruba and Hausa, each of which is currently spoken by some 25 million people.

Most early writings in African languages were prayers, hymns, and religious texts. For example, one of the first books to appear in Grebo (spoken in Liberia) was a hymn book, printed more than 150 years ago.

Popular themes in West African-language literature in the 20th century included Christianity, tradition, myths, and the supernatural. Recently, there has been a

African-language drama is widely used in Africa for teaching purposes. Important themes treated by theater groups include health awareness and good citizenship. Here, a play group teaches civic education to refugees from the long-running conflict in Sierra Leone in the late 1990s.

Another major contributor to West African-language theater was Duro Ladipo (1931–78), whose groundbreaking folk operas (such as *Oba Koso* and *Eda*) were performed to great acclaim at several European festivals in the 1960s. These operas are based on incidents from Yoruba history, and incorporate dialog, ritual poetry, dance routines, and traditional rhythms played on African musical instruments such as the *bata* drum.

NOVELS

The first work of fiction to appear in Yoruba was *Sègilolá eléyinjú egé* (Segilola of the Seductive Eyes) by Isaac Babalola Thomas. This tale, which deals with issues of prostitution and morality, first appeared in serial form in a local newspaper in 1929. Daniel Olorunfemi Fagunwa (1903–63), who also wrote in Yoruba, actively promoted Christian teachings, while also making extensive use of traditional forms such as proverbs and folklore. His most famous works narrate the heroic journeys undertaken by Yoruba hunters.

The first book to be published in Igbo was *Omenuko* (1933) by Pita Nwana. This prize-winning tale of a slave trader remained a best seller for many decades.

SEE ALSO: *African religions; English-language literature; Hausa; Islam; Oral literature.*

trend away from fantasy toward greater realism, with writers focusing on such themes as political corruption, the challenges of modern life, and family relations.

In 2000, African writers and scholars held the conference Against All Odds at Asmara, Eritrea, to celebrate the vitality of African languages and literatures. The conference pledged to foster future African-language literature throughout the continent.

PLAYS

West African-language theater owes much to the pioneering work of Hubert Ogunde (b.1916) who, in the 1940s, wrote plays in both English and Yoruba and formed Nigeria's first theater company. Efua Sutherland (1924–96) played a similar role in the theater scene in Ghana, when she founded the Experimental Theatre Company (later the Ghana Drama Studio) in Accra in 1958. This paved the way for the Ghana National Theatre in Accra, which has since become a lively center for theatrical and musical productions.

AFRICAN LANGUAGES AND LITERATURE
Linguists estimate that out of approximately 1,000 African languages, fewer than 10 percent can boast any significant written literature. A number of different factors have hindered the development of literature in these languages. First and foremost, many African languages still have no standardized written form. In other words, there is no broad agreement on grammar, or the spelling, tone, or pronunciation of certain words. The number of different dialects that exist in most languages has also made standardization impossible. In addition, many West African authors are deterred from writing in local languages since that would seriously restrict their readership and their income.

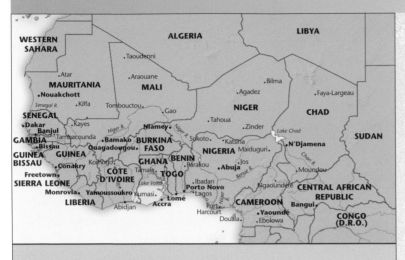

FACT FILE

Population	Ghana 8 million; Côte d'Ivoire up to 7 million
Religion	Christianity; Akan religions; Islam
Language	Various Akan languages and dialects, such as Asante Twi, Fante Twi, or Kwahu (all from the Proto-Kwa branch of the Niger-Congo family).

TIMELINE

c.1400	Kingdom of Bono, the earliest Akan kingdom, emerges.
1471	First contact between Europeans (Portuguese) and the Akan.
1482	The Portuguese build São Jorge da Mina (Elmina) Castle on land loaned from the Akan as a permanent trading post; it becomes a major site of the slave trade.
1600s–1800	The Gold Coast area (present-day southern Ghana) becomes an area of intense British–Dutch rivalry.
1807	Slave trade is abolished throughout the British Empire.
1878	Cocoa is introduced to Ghana by Tetteh Quashie.
1896	The Asante are defeated and King Prempeh I is exiled by the British, who declare a protectorate over Asante.
1899–1900	Last Anglo-Asante war; the Asante are finally defeated and their leader, Yaa Asantewaa, is exiled.
1902	Asante is formally declared a British crown colony.
1957	The Gold Coast becomes the first African colony to gain independence, with Kwame Nkrumah as leader.
1966	Nkrumah is overthrown in a military coup.
1979	Flight-Lieutenant Jerry Rawlings leads a coup in Ghana, stages another (Second Coming) in 1981, and stays in power for almost 20 years.
2000	The Rawlings era ends as John Agyekum Kufuor is elected president of Ghana.

THE AKAN HAVE BEEN RENOWNED FOR MINING AND CRAFTING GOLD. ONE AKAN SUBGROUP, THE ASANTE, BUILT A STRONG AND PROSPEROUS EMPIRE THAT LASTED UNTIL THE EARLY YEARS OF THE 20TH CENTURY.

HISTORY

The ancestors of the Akan peoples migrated from more northerly regions into the forest and coastal areas of present-day Ghana and eastern Côte d'Ivoire in around the 13th century.

The Akan people are made up of a number of distinct groups. When the Portuguese first arrived in the region in the 15th century, they came into contact with an Akan subgroup known as the Fante, who had settled along the coast. The most prominent of the Akan ethnic subgroups, however, were the Asante (or Ashanti). Partly through military conquests (in many cases of other Akan subgroups) and partly through absorbing weaker peoples, the Asante created the Asante empire, which grew steadily throughout the 17th and 18th century. Its king (asantehene) Osei Tutu, who ruled at the beginning of the 18th century, was responsible for its greatest period of expansion. Asante survived as an imperial power until the end of the 19th century, when, following a series of conflicts (known as the Asante wars), it was conquered by the British.

DAILY LIFE AND SOCIETY

Although the subgroups that make up the Akan all have common origins, they remain distinct units, since they speak different languages and dialects and have different cultural practices and identities.

Historically, most of the Akan subgroups were organized matrilineally (that is, tracing

Akan from Côte d'Ivoire conduct a ritual to purify one of the ancestral stools of this people. Such ceremonies are common to all the Akan subgroups. Most famously, the Golden Stool of the Asante embodies the nation's soul, and was hidden from the British when they annexed the empire in 1902.

descent through the female line). The extended family remains a very important social institution, although many families today, particularly in urban areas, are adopting the Western model of living in a nuclear family.

In the past, the Akan mostly worked in subsistence farming or fishing—that is, to supply their own immediate needs. Since colonial times, cocoa had been grown for export; this important crop was introduced in the late 19th century by Tetteh Quashie, a Ghanaian returning from the then-Spanish island of Fernando Póo (Bioko). In modern Ghana, most Akan are still farmers, although a growing number are migrating to cities such as Kumasi or Accra in search of work.

CULTURE AND RELIGION

The Akan religion focuses on a supreme being and also involves many lesser gods and spirits who are endowed with varying degrees of supernatural power. The spirits of the ancestors are thought to be ever-present and can be called upon by people for help.

Today, most Akan are strongly Christian, especially in urban areas. The main denominations are Anglican, Methodist, Roman Catholic, and Presbyterian, although many new evangelical churches are also emerging in the big cities. Some Akan have adopted Islam. However, the Asante royalty still follow the Asante religion, as part of their role in upholding Asante culture. This centers on the worship of a supreme god known as *Nyame*.

SEE ALSO: *Architecture; Christianity; Festival and ceremony; Funeral and reliquary art; Marriage and the family; Metalwork; Sculpture; Textiles.*

THE ADINKRA SYMBOLS

The Adinkra symbols were traditionally signs used by the Asante, although they now appear all over southern Ghana. The most common of them is the Gye Nyame symbol (right), which literally means Only God and represents the supremacy of God. This symbol is commonly seen on house fronts and shop signs or on printed fabrics, clothes, and jewelry.

NOTABLE WEST AFRICAN BUILDINGS

City	Country	Building
Djenné	Mali	Great Mosque
Kano	Nigeria	Emir's Palace
Zaria	Nigeria	Friday Mosque
Tombouctou	Mali	Djinguereber Mosque
Gao	Mali	Tomb of Askia Muhammad
Agadez	Niger	Great Mosque
Yamoussoukro	Côte d'Ivoire	Basilica of Our Lady of Peace

AS MIGHT BE EXPECTED FROM SUCH A LARGE AND DIVERSE AREA, WEST AFRICA HAS AN ENORMOUS VARIETY OF ARCHITECTURAL STYLES. BUILDINGS RANGE FROM CITY WALLS SEVERAL MILES LONG AND LARGE PUBLIC BUILDINGS SUCH AS MOSQUES TO HOUSES, WHICH ARE TYPICALLY ARRANGED INTO FAMILY LIVING GROUPS, OR COMPOUNDS.

The Great Mosque at Djenné in Mali was rebuilt in 1907 on the site of a mosque that had existed since the 13th century. It is built in the style introduced into the Sahel by Islam. The walls are constructed from dried clay reinforced with wooden beams.

There is also considerable diversity in the building materials used, which are mainly determined by geography. However, across the region one growing trend is the use of modern materials such as cement and corrugated iron.

THE SAHARA

In the Sahara, which has long been home to peoples with a nomadic lifestyle, dwellings must be portable and easy to dismantle. Although it can be very hot during the daytime, it can also get extremely cold at night. Fabric and leather are suitably light and impermanent materials. Flexible branches (typically bent into domes) are also used; however, since trees are rare in this environment, wood is used sparingly.

A typical sight in the Sahara is a Tuareg family on the move,

the mosques and Quranic libraries at Chinguetti in Mauritania—but is now rare. Adobe architecture, which developed in the flood plains on the Niger river where plentiful mud was available for construction, is represented most famously by the Great Mosque at Djenné in Mali, with its tall towers and protruding wooden beams (see ISLAM). Adobe buildings vary between different Sahel towns, but are generally referred to as being built in the Sudanic style, namely under the influence of the Muslim cultures to the north and the east. Other examples of this style from farther east in the Sahel are the Hausa-inspired timber-framed emir's palace at Kano (Nigeria) and the mosque at Agadez (Niger).

Quite distinct from buildings in this Islamic-inspired style are the heavily decorated houses found in parts of Burkina Faso.

FOREST REGIONS

Historically, buildings in the rainforest areas in the south of the region are built on a framework of wood with adobe walls and roofs made of palm fronds, straw thatch, or wood. The compounds of the Asante in central Ghana and the Yoruba in southwestern Nigeria were constructed in this way, with several houses surrounding a central courtyard. Concrete and corrugated iron sheeting are now increasingly used in such buildings.

Western influence on architecture in the region is apparent, for example, in the Creole style adopted in buildings put up by former slaves who came from the New World to settle in Freetown in Sierra Leone. Similarly, architectural elements from the southern states of the United States, such as verandahs (Plantation style), were incorporated into buildings by the freed American slaves who settled in Liberia.

with their donkeys carrying intricately carved wooden bed feet (placed under the bed to insulate the sleeper from the heat or cold of the desert floor).

THE SAHEL

Two features characterize architecture in the Sahel (the southern semidesert fringe of the Sahara): the use of adobe (sun-baked mud) as a building material and the influence of Islam. In pre-colonial times, stone was often used for important buildings—for example

No expense was spared in constructing the massive Basilica of our Lady of Peace at Yamoussoukro in Côte d'Ivoire. Marble was imported from Italy and stained glass from France. The building costs doubled the country's national debt. Only one-third of Ivoirians are Catholic.

THE LARGEST CHURCH IN THE WORLD
Over a period of just four years (1986–90) Félix Houphouët-Boigny, president of Côte d'Ivoire between 1960 and 1993, had a colossal Roman Catholic cathedral built in his birthplace, Yamoussoukro. A virtual replica of St. Peter's in Rome, the Basilica of Our Lady of Peace was consecrated by Pope John Paul II in 1990. With a total surface of 322,800 sq ft (29,988 sq m, or more than five and a half American football fields), it is the largest church in the world. It stands 551 ft (168 meters) tall, and can seat 7,000 people in the nave with standing room for an additional 12,000. The building cost $150 million (supposedly from the president's own funds) and caused great controversy for such a poor country.

SEE ALSO: Akan; Islam; Tuareg; Yoruba.

CHRISTIANITY

TIMELINE

15th century	The first Christian missionaries, traveling on board Portuguese ships, arrive in West Africa, but few people convert.
1700–1711	The first European trans-Saharan crossing to Katsina (from Tripoli in present-day Libya) is made by a Franciscan missionary, but goes largely unrecorded.
18th century	Returning slaves from Britain and the Caribbean settle in Sierra Leone and spread Christianity.
19th century	Europeans and Americans began to install mission stations throughout Africa.
1962–65	Roman Catholic Vatican Council II encourages the growth of African Catholic clergy and more popular forms of worship.

CHRISTIANITY ONLY REACHED WEST AFRICA IN THE 15TH CENTURY WHEN PORTUGUESE SAILORS LANDED ON THE ATLANTIC COAST. NOW, CHRISTIANITY IN ITS MANY DIVERSE FORMS IS ONE OF THE MOST WIDELY PRACTICED RELIGIONS OF THE REGION.

HISTORY

In the late 18th century, former African slaves freed by the British began to settle in the colony of Freetown, in what is now Sierra Leone. This colony had been set up by British antislavery campaigners. There, the freed slaves sowed the seed of a new phase of West African Christianity. The American ex-slaves who populated Liberia from 1847 onward were also devout Christians who belonged to Episcopal, Methodist, or Baptist

THE HARRIST CHURCH

The Kru people of Liberia and Côte d'Ivoire were among the earliest groups in Africa to be converted en masse to Christianity. This came about through the efforts of William Wadé Harris (c.1865–1929), a Grebo from Liberia, who worked for the American Episcopal mission there. Called in a vision to become a preacher, he founded an evangelical movement called the Harrist Church and traveled along the West African coast with his message from 1913 onward. He succeeded in converting more than 120,000 people.

The fastest growing churches throughout Africa—and West Africa is no exception—are the independent evangelical churches. Their charismatic forms of worship attract many followers, such as these worshippers at at open-air prayer meeting in Benin City, Nigeria.

churches. Efforts to Christianize Africa were boosted in the 19th century by the establishment there of European and American mission stations. Yet it was only by the end of that century, when they were supported by colonial governments, that they ventured far into the interior—a region that, in West Africa, had long been strongly Islamic. The condemnation of polygamy (having several wives) by non-African Christian missionaries was a major barrier to the spread of the faith, since many rulers were unwilling to abandon this practice. Though many of the early independent Christian churches, especially in West Africa, believed polygamy to be essentially African, most African Christians now reject polygamy.

MODERN WEST AFRICAN CHRISTIANITY

The end of colonialism across Africa in the 1960s coincided with a new attitude toward African Christianity by the Western mother churches. The Roman Catholic Vatican Council II, which generally modernized the faith, had a great impact on African Catholicism. More popular forms of worship took root (such as using African music and instrumentation for singing hymns) and many African priests were ordained. Indeed, Africans are now prominent in missions worldwide; with more practicing Christians than any other continent, Africa is at the forefront of spreading the faith. A similar development has occurred in the Anglican church, where West African bishops now

form a dynamic, evangelical lobby. Many are traditionalists, who are united in their opposition to the ordination of gay clergy.

There is a broad spectrum of Christianity in West Africa today, embracing Roman Catholic, Protestant, and African independent churches. The latter range from versions of Western Protestant churches to Christian versions of African religions. One large grouping of such churches in West Africa is known as Aladura, from the Yoruba word meaning "a person who prays." In addition to their stress on the effectiveness of prayer (especially in healing the sick), followers also believe in the power of the Holy Spirit. Though some of the more exuberant and spirit-based forms of worship may resemble those of African religions, members of the church are strongly opposed to the witchcraft they identify in traditional medicine. The independent Christian churches of West Africa have experienced a phenomenal rate of growth, and now claim more than 20 million followers.

SEE ALSO: African religions; African-language literature; Akan; Architecture; Festival and ceremony; Islam; Marriage and the family.

SAMUEL AJAYI CROWTHER

Samuel Ajayi Crowther (1807–91) was born in Osogun in Yorubaland, Nigeria. He was captured and enslaved at the age of 13, but was rescued by a British antislavery patrol and resettled in the colony of Sierra Leone. After being baptized and educated, Crowther won renown for his work as a Christian teacher and missionary. In 1864, he was the first African to be ordained as a bishop, being appointed as head of the Church of England in West Africa. Yet despite Crowther's great success in winning many converts, conservative forces criticized his appointment, and after his death ensured that no more Africans attained high office. This snub stimulated the growth of independent African churches.

CONTEMPORARY ART AND PHOTOGRAPHY

ARTISTS IN WEST AFRICA

Artist	Dates	Country	Medium
Seydou Keita	b.1923	Mali	Photography
Malick Sidibé	b.1935	Mali	Photography
Jimoh Buraimoh	b.1943	Nigeria	Painting
El Anatsui	b.1944	Ghana	Sculpture
Twins Seven Seven	b.1945	Nigeria	Painting
Ndidi Dike	b.1958	Nigeria	Sculpture
Chika Aneke	b.1978	Nigeria	Sculpture

NO LESS THAN MODERN ART FROM OTHER PARTS OF THE WORLD, CONTEMPORARY WORKS OF ART FROM WEST AFRICA ARE DRIVEN BY THE CREATIVE VISION OF THEIR INDIVIDUAL MAKERS. YET THEY ALSO DRAW ON A LONG HISTORY OF ARTISTIC ENDEAVOR IN THE REGION, WHOSE PRODUCTS WERE NOT JUST "ART FOR ART'S SAKE" BUT OFTEN HAD A DEEPER SPIRITUAL SIGNIFICANCE AND SOCIAL PURPOSE.

One of Malick Sidibé's candid photographs of Malian life in the 1960s shows a young man dancing the twist at a party. Sidibé came to international attention in 1995, but his work had been known in West Africa for decades.

West Africa's contemporary artists are busy reinterpreting and reworking this rich legacy. Using a variety of traditional and nontraditional media, the subjects their works embody range from the personal to the national, and beyond. One enduring modern theme is the question of African identity in the postcolonial period.

An important movement in modern West African art was the Oshogbo school, named for the town in southwestern Nigeria where it developed from the early 1960s onward. One of its founder members, who went on to achieve fame in Africa and worldwide, is the painter and musician Twins Seven Seven (b.1945). His vibrant etchings, oil paintings, and mixed media works revolve around the legends and ceremonies of the Yoruba people. Other notable painters of this school include Jimoh Buraimoh (b.1943) and Yinka Adeyemi (b.1941). Buraimoh is known for his unique style of bead-painting, while Adeyemi's work celebrates the rich mythological heritage of the Yoruba.

PICTURING THE NEW AFRICA

Malick Sidibé (b.1935) from Mali is one of the best-known African photographers. Having first trained in painting and design, he opened his own photographic studio in Bamako in 1962, where people came to have their picture taken on special occasions such as weddings, initiations, or the birth of their children. Sidibé's photos pioneered a new image of Africa, with none of the patronizing clichés of colonialism. Rather, he showed the fellow citizens of his newly independent homeland as confident, cosmopolitan individuals.

used as posts to support verandahs, that comment on contemporary political and social life. The young sculptor Chika Aneke has created painted wooden and mixed-media pieces on such topical themes as the computer revolution and the 9/11 terrorist attacks.

Photography as an art form does not have a long history in West Africa, and is only just starting to become an important medium for communicating ideas. Bamako, the capital of Mali, is becoming a major center for African photography. This city is home to the famous photographers Seydou Keita (b.1923), Malick Sidibé (see box feature), and Alioune Bâ (b.1959) and a major gallery specializing in photography, the Gallery Chab. Bamako also hosts the African Photography Encounters exhibition every two years. An exciting workshop project for the 2005 event is "Visual Griots," which encourages Malian children to tell their communities' stories through photography.

INFLUENCE BEYOND WEST AFRICA

African art first came to the attention of the European public in around 1905, when artists began to recognize the expressive power and beautiful simplicity of West African sculpture. Many artists, such as the French "Fauvists" Vlaminck and Derain, and the Italian sculptor and painter Modigliani, were fascinated by African art forms and owned collections of masks from Côte d'Ivoire. Most famously, the Spanish painter Pablo Picasso was strongly influenced by masks of the Dogon people of Mali when he created his groundbreaking Cubist picture *Les Demoiselles d'Avignon* in 1907. These early 20th-century artists were intrigued by what they patronisingly saw as the "primitive" qualities of African art, to shock their contemporary audience. Since then, interest in the arts of Africa has grown.

Sculpture has long been regarded as one of Africa's most distinctive art forms. Notable modern sculptors include the Ghanaian Ewe artist El Anatsui (b.1944) and the Nigerians Ndidi Dike and Chika Aneke. El Anatsui is well-known for his large pieces using innovative techniques, such as carving wood with a chainsaw or assembling discarded items such as bottle tops into brightly colored panels. The artist Ndidi Dike is known for her adaptations of African art forms, for example totem poles

A modern mural showing slaves, in the village of Juffure in Gambia. This place became famous when U.S. author Alex Haley traced his ancestor there, in the novel Roots *(see* FESTIVAL AND CEREMONY*).*

SEE ALSO: *Festival and ceremony; Funeral and reliquary art; Leatherwork; Masks and masquerade; Metalwork; Sculpture; Textiles.*

DANCE AND SONG

DANCE COMPANIES AND STYLES

Company/style	Country
5ème Dimension	Senegal
Artea	Senegal
Le Ballet National la Linguère	Senegal
Les Ballets Africains	Guinea
Gumbe	Guinea-Bissau
Lamba	Mali

The African tradition of performing music and dance to honor leaders continues to the present day. Here, dancers of the Lorma people (a Mande subgroup) from Tubmanburg, Liberia stage a dance to welcome Sekouh Conneh, leader of one of the guerrilla groups fighting for control of the country, in 2003.

DANCE IS EXTREMELY IMPORTANT IN AFRICAN CULTURES. PEOPLE DANCE AT EVERY CEREMONY. DANCE IS USED TO MARK SOCIAL EVENTS AND LEARNING. IT CELEBRATES BIRTH, PUBERTY, GOOD HARVESTS, MARRIAGES, AND DEATHS. DANCE IS ONE OF THE PRINCIPAL WAYS IN WHICH WEST AFRICAN PEOPLES EXPRESS THEIR CULTURAL IDENTITY AND KEEP IN TOUCH WITH THEIR CULTURAL HERITAGE.

The traditional dances of West Africa include *gumbe*, a harvest dance, *lamba*, a dance of celebration, and *sunu*, performed at weddings. *Gumbe* is particularly associated with the small country of Guineau-Bissau, and describes a musical style with complex, catchy rhythms played on a water-drum accompanying a sensual, salsa-like dance. It originated among slaves in Jamaica, and came back to West Africa as part of the Creole culture. The Mande dance the *lamba* to honor the ancestors and to give thanks for good fortune; it is also linked to the *griots* (storytellers). Malian women perform the *sunu* (literally meaning "young woman") in anticipation of a future wedding. The Ewe and the Yoruba have long-standing traditions of dance–drumming at their festivals.

Modern West African dance retains many traditional elements, but is also open to influence by modern forms. In its turn, it has influenced dance forms from other continents, with African dance companies making international tours. In some countries of the region, such as Senegal, Mali, and Guinea, professional dance has been strongly promoted, and new dance companies established with state support. Les Ballets Africains from Guinea, led by

Fodeba Keita, are considered one of the best African dance companies, and have been touring the world for almost 50 years. They perform a mix of traditional dance and music, as well as acrobatics, comedy, and drama. Senegal is also home to a number of other dance companies that explore indigenous dance traditions and blend them with elements of modern dance.

SONG

The Tuareg and the Hausa are leading exponents of the traditional song in West Africa. Among the Tuareg, men and women practice separate forms and styles of singing. Women's songs of praise, exorcism, and dance are accompanied by goat-skin (*tinde*) or camel-skin (*tabl*) drums or others made from half-gourds floating upside down in water. Men's songs, performed solo, may be unaccompanied, but are often partnered by the *inzad*, a single-stringed fiddle. Hausa music shows a different kind of division, between ceremonial court music on the one hand and the music of rural people on the other. The former is performed (often by noblemen) on state occasions for sultans and emirs, with large state trumpets, horns, and drums used as symbols of royal authority. Songs of praise for rulers are usually accompanied by percussion instruments— either small kettledrums or talking drums. Traditional rural singing, now disappearing, made wide use of drums and fiddles.

As modern global influences obscure regional variety, it is vital that traditional song forms be recorded for posterity. In the late 1950s, the young guitarist Ali Farka Touré (b.1939), later to become world-famous as the African bluesman, accompanied the writer Amadou Hampâté Ba (see FULANI) on a journey around their native Mali, using a tape recorder to record the songs of rural people. Touré's cataloging of the traditional sounds of Mali not only enriched his own musical range, but also performed an invaluable service in helping preserve his country's musical heritage.

The renowned Guinean dance and music company Les Ballets Africains have been delighting audiences worldwide with their performances since 1958. They are seen here on stage in Los Angeles; the musician on the left is playing the kora, *a West African harp made from a gourd (calabash).*

SEE ALSO: *Fulani; Hausa; Music and musical instruments; Oral literature; Tuareg.*

DANCE COMPANY 5ÈME DIMENSION

This innovative Senegalese dance company was founded in 1995 by Jean Tamba, a young professor of dance from the Dakar Conservatory, and a cultural activist, Honoré Mendy. The company has developed new creations, and has toured extensively abroad. They have researched contemporary African dance extensively, and used their knowledge to devise a new fusion style that they call *mestizo dance.*

DOGON

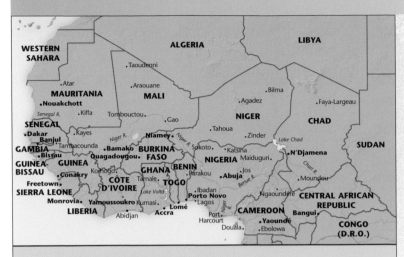

FACT FILE

Population	Mali 500,000
Religion	Dogon religion, Islam
Language	Dogon. A member of the Niger-Congo family, Dogon has many dialects, often virtually unintelligible to one another.

TIMELINE

14th–15th centuries	Raids by the cavalry of the Mossi drive the ancestors of the Dogon westward to settle around the Bandiagara escarpment in what is now Mali.
1700–1750	The Mossi kingdoms of Katenga (Ouahigouya) and Ouagadougou become the dominant regional powers on the Central Volta plateau.
17th–18th centuries	The slave-raiding Bambara kingdoms of Ségou and Kaarta grow on either side of the Niger River, causing conflict in the Bandiagara area.
1818–97	The Islamic Macina state is founded in the inner Niger Delta by the Fulani reformer Sekou Amadou; a jihad led by Tukulor (sedentary Fulani) Umar Tal leads to the occupation of most of Mali. Both conflicts result in Dogon conversion or emigration to the hills.
1897–1920	Ongoing period of French colonization is completed with the submission of the last Dogon village in 1920.
1960	Mali gains independence.
1968	General Moussa Traoré seizes power in Mali in a military coup.
1980–present	Dogon country becomes a major tourist draw for Mali. The area is listed as a UNESCO world heritage site in 1989.
1991	General Traoré deposed as leader of Mali in a bloodless military coup.

THE DOGON OF CENTRAL MALI ARE RENOWNED FOR THEIR INTRICATE WOODCARVINGS AND THEIR COMPLEX KNOWLEDGE OF THE STARS AND THE UNIVERSE. MANY DOGON SETTLEMENTS ARE LOCATED IN REMOTE RAVINES ALONG THE BANDIAGARA CLIFFS, A LINE OF SANDSTONE ESCARPMENTS 125 MILES (200 KM) LONG AND UP TO 2,000 FEET (600 M) ABOVE SEA LEVEL.

HISTORY

The ancestors of the Dogon are thought to have taken refuge in mountainous regions while fleeing from armed conflicts, slave raids, or forcible religious conversion. According to oral history, the Dogon were probably a mix of groups with different origins that reached the Bandiagara cliffs in the early 14th century C.E. They replaced the local inhabitants (Tellem), who made some of the earliest textiles in sub-Saharan Africa.

The Dogon have had a succession of powerful states as their neighbors, from the Empire of Mali in the 1200s–1400s to the present-day Republic of Mali. While they have absorbed some outside influences they have rejected others. Variations among the Dogon in language, material culture, oral traditions, and social and ritual institutions reveal much about their checkered history.

SOCIETY AND DAILY LIFE

The Dogon are primarily crop growers who farm the sparse land available to them intensively, cutting terraces into the steep slopes. They grow millet, corn, and onions, and they also keep goat and sheep herds.

The basic residential unit is the family household (*gina*), usually composed of a man, his wife or wives, and their unmarried children. The term *gina* is also applied to the

THE LEWE FERTILITY CULT

The cult of Lewe, the earth god, is related to the agricultural cycle and is observed in every Dogon village at shrines specially dedicated to this deity. The cult's chief priest, usually the oldest man in the village, is known as a *hogon*. The Dogon believe that Lewe visits the *hogon* every night in the form of a snake, which licks the priest's skin to purify him and instil the life force into him. The *hogon* officiates at agricultural ceremonies and is responsible for maintaining the purity of the soil; the altars in Lewe shrines incorporate lumps of earth to ensure the continued fertility of the land.

"great house" occupied by the family head. Dogon villages are organized according to a system of extended families, or lineages. Each of these lineages owns separate houses and fields and has its own shrines, rituals, and burial plot. The lineage head (a male elder) leads the worship of the ancestors and presides over a council settling family disputes, managing property, and sending delegates to the village council. Groups of individuals of a similar age ("age-grades") are another important feature of Dogon social life. All community members must undergo several rites of passage during their lifetime.

Within each village, there are specialist craftspeople such as blacksmiths, leatherworkers, and bards (griots), each with their particular spiritual beliefs.

CULTURE AND RELIGION

Dogon social organization, material culture and beliefs have witnessed considerable change over the last 100 years. This has mainly come about as a result of the influence of Islam. However, although now eclipsed by Islam, ancestral Dogon religion is well documented. It centers on three gods: Amma, the sky god and creator of the world; Nommo, the water god; and Lewe (or Lebe), the earth god. The religion is closely bound up with Dogon culture and daily life; shrines and sacred

A Dogon village on the Bandiagara escarpment, Mali. The distinctive pepperpot-shaped buildings are granaries for storing millet, supported on stones to stop rats and mice getting in.

objects are features of Dogon villages. Moreover, the layout of villages and of individual houses mirrors Dogon perceptions of the world. For example, the ground plan of Dogon houses is modeled on the human body, and the relative positions of buildings symbolizes how Amma created the world.

Dogon ceremonies typically take place after the harvest, between March and May. A major festival, the *Dama*, bids farewell to those who have died and can last several days. The *Sigui* ceremony, at which dances are performed telling the story of Dogon origins, is held every 60 years. Its date is determined when the star Sirius is thought to be in a favorable position. Masks play an important role in religious ceremonies—the Dogon have no fewer than 78 different types of ritual masks. Among the most famous of these are the *kanaga* (see MASKS AND MASQUERADE) and the *iminana*, in the shape of a snake with a headpiece up to 30 feet (9 m) tall. The use of masks is rooted in history, but the tradition is not static: some masks are discarded and new ones introduced.

SEE ALSO: Fulani, Masks and masquerade; Metalwork; Mossi; Oral literature.

MAJOR WORKS AND THEIR AUTHORS

Title	Date	Author	Country
The Interesting Narrative of the Life of Olaudah Equiano	1789	Olaudah Equiano	Nigeria/UK
A Dictionary of the Yoruba Language	1843	Samuel Ajayi Crowther	Nigeria
West Africa before Europe	1905	Edward Blyden	Liberia
Ethiopia Unbound	1911	Joseph Ephraim Casely-Hayford	Ghana
The Palm-Wine Drinkard	1952	Amos Tutuola	Nigeria
Things Fall Apart	1958	Chinua Achebe	Nigeria
The Beautiful Ones are not yet Born	1968	Ayi Kwei Armah	Ghana
Changes – A Love Story	1991	Ama Ata Aidoo	Ghana
The Famished Road	1992	Ben Okri	Nigeria
From Zia, with Love	1992	Wole Soyinka	Nigeria

WEST AFRICAN LITERATURE IN ENGLISH BEGAN IN THE 18TH CENTURY. THESE EARLY WRITINGS TOOK THE FORM OF RELIGIOUS TEXTS, POLITICAL TRACTS, OR AUTOBIOGRAPHIES, WHOSE AUTHORS WERE MOSTLY FREED SLAVES. YET IT WAS NOT UNTIL THE SPREAD OF EDUCATION IN THE 20TH CENTURY THAT ENGLISH-LANGUAGE LITERATURE REALLY TOOK ROOT AND SIGNIFICANT NUMBERS OF POETS, NOVELISTS, AND DRAMATISTS BEGAN TO EMERGE.

The frontispiece of Olaudah Equiano's autobiography. This work was the first to describe the hardships of a slave's life, and became a bestseller. Nine editions were published before Equiano's death in 1797.

EARLY THEMES

Poems and novels from the 1950s and 1960s were heavily influenced by the tempos and rhythms of the oral traditions of West Africa. For example, in his first novel *The Voice* (1964), the Nigerian writer Gabriel Okara (b.1921) translated directly from his own language, Ijaw; even the structure of his English sentences followed Ijaw syntax. Similarly, the Ghanaian poet and novelist Kofi Awoonor (b.1935) modeled much of his early work on the traditional form of Ewe oral poetry known as dirge singing, of which his grandmother was a leading

OLAUDAH EQUIANO

The author and antislavery campaigner Olaudah Equiano (c.1745–97; also known as Gustavus Vassa) was one of the founding fathers of African English-language literature. His 1789 autobiography *The Interesting Narrative of the Life of Olaudah Equiano*, tells of his adventurous life, starting with his childhood in a village in the Igbo lands of southern Nigeria. There, he was kidnapped by a slave-raiding party and shipped first to Barbados in the West Indies, and then to Virginia in the United States. Sold to an English naval officer, he learned to read and write and saw action in naval battles between the British and French. Eventually, he managed to buy his freedom and settled in London.

performer. In a poem in his first collection *Rediscovery* (1964), Awoonor used the image of the weaverbird, which destroys the tree it nests in, as a symbol of the damage created in Africa by colonialism.

Common early themes were the new sense of national pride following independence, and the legacy of colonialism. One writer who explored such themes was the Ghanaian author Ayi Kwei Armah, whose novel *The Beautiful Ones are not yet Born* (1968) exposed greed and corruption in Ghana.

POETRY AND PLAYS

The number of poems and plays written in English increased greatly in the last decades of the 20th century. Writers such as Wole Soyinka (b.1934) and Femi Osofisan (b.1946) from Nigeria, and Ama Ata Aidoo (b.1942) from Ghana (who also writes novels and short stories) have won worldwide acclaim for their poetry and drama. These writers often build on the work of earlier authors by using oral traditions and African literary forms based on storytelling or dancing. They also explore new themes such as sexual politics, the manipulation of the mass media, and ethnicity. Wole Soyinka was awarded the Nobel Prize for Literature in 1986.

NOVELS AND SHORT STORIES

One of the key inspirations for many English-language writers in West Africa is local folklore and mythology. For example,

in *The Palm-Wine Drinkard* and *My Life in the Bush of Ghosts* (both from 1952) the Nigerian writer Amos Tutuola (1920–97) was strongly influenced by Yoruba mythology in his creation of fictional worlds full of magic and inhabited by spirits.

Contemporary West African English-language literature is dominated by Nigerian writers. Chinua Achebe (b.1930) is the author of *Things Fall Apart* (1958), *Arrow of God* (1964), and *Anthills of the Savannah* (1987), which investigate the impact of colonialism and African cultures. His younger compatriot Ben Okri (b.1959) has written many "magical realist" novels, short stories, and poems. Okri's favorite themes are corruption, poverty, and violence in Nigeria, as well as the clash between foreign and indigenous cultures in Africa.

A production of the Nigerian writer Wole Soyinka's play The Road. *Nobel prize winner Soyinka was imprisoned for his peace activism during the Biafran War (1967–70). His novels and dramas frequently criticize state oppression and corruption.*

SEE ALSO: *African-language literature; French-language literature; Movies; Oral literature.*

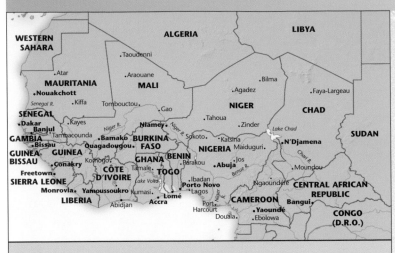

FACT FILE

Population Ghana c.2.2 million; Togo c.2 million;
Benin 200,000

Religion Christianity, Ewe religion, Islam

Language Ewe, which belongs to the Proto-Kwa group
of the Niger-Congo family of languages, has a
number of different dialects, including Anlo Ewe,
spoken in Ghana.

TIMELINE

c.1500 The Ewe settle in the town of Notsé (in modern Togo).

c.1600 The Ewe quit Notsé, fleeing from King Agakoli's tyranny.

1847 German missionaries arrive in Ewe territory.

1898 Almost all of West Africa is occupied by the colonies
of European powers (mainly France and Britain).

1922 Togoland divided between Britain and France after
German defeat in World War I (1914–18).

1956 English-administered Trans-Volta region votes in a
referendum to be included in Ghana on independence.

1957 Ghana is the first sub-Saharan African country
to win independence.

1960 Togo and Dahomey become independent from France.

1967 Gnassingbé Eyadema seizes power in Togo.

1972 Mathieu Kérékou seizes power in Dahomey
(renamed Benin in 1975).

1979 Jerry Rawlings, the son of an Ewe mother and a
Scottish father, stages a military coup in Ghana.

2000 John Agyekum Kufuor is elected president of Ghana.

2005 Gnassingbé Eyadema dies and his son Faure
Gnassingbé is elected president of Togo.

THE EWE, WHO ARE CLOSELY RELATED TO THE FON, ARE THOUGHT TO HAVE MIGRATED TO WEST AFRICA FROM THE NORTH AROUND 500 YEARS AGO. THE LACK OF STRONG POLITICAL UNITY—LATER REINFORCED BY THE ARBITRARY COLONIAL FRONTIERS—HAS LEFT THE EWE DISPERSED ACROSS THREE PRESENT-DAY STATES: GHANA, TOGO, AND BENIN.

HISTORY

After first settling in the area around the town of Notsé in modern Togo, the Ewe were persecuted and fled from this area. Following their dispersal, the Ewe settled farther west. As a result the Ewe are a confederation of subgroups split into independent chieftaincies rather than a single unit. The Ewe's initial contact with Europeans was hostile, as they fought against Danish traders who had built forts on the eastern Gold Coast. Thereafter, however, the Ewe traded slaves and later coconuts and palm oil with the Europeans.

In the late 19th century, the western Ewe came under British rule in the colony of the Gold Coast (Ghana), while the Germans ruled the eastern Ewe in Togoland.

SOCIETY AND DAILY LIFE

In the past, village economies were based on farming, hunting, fishing, weaving, and market trading. These activities are still very common, although education and urbanization have given many Ewe access to new types of employment.

An Ewe dancer from Mepe, in the Volta region of Ghana, performs the ceremonial atumpan dance. Originally relating to war and danced only by male warriors, this dance is now performed by both men and women.

The structure of a standard household was formerly based on a male head with a wife, children, and an extended family of unmarried or elderly relatives. Today, the make-up of Ewe households is more varied as a result of changes associated with education, Christianity, and the migration of men to cities in search of work.

CULTURE AND RELIGION

Dance–drumming, including both hand drumming and stick drumming, is an integral part of community and religious life among the Ewe. It is still widely practiced at funerals and ceremonies, and many of the dance-drumming repertoires have evolved to reflect modern cultural values.

Most Ewe are officially Christian, although in many areas their Christian faith incorporates some elements of the pre-Christian Ewe religion. The Ewe religion is based on the worship of a supreme being (Mawuga Kitikata) and lesser gods, and the veneration of ancestors.

SEE ALSO: Festival and ceremony; Fon; Masks and masquerade; Music and musical instruments; Textiles.

THE FLIGHT FROM NOTSÉ

According to oral history, the Ewe fled the town of Notsé because of the cruel treatment they suffered at the hands of King Agakoli. Their escape was organized by an old man called Tegli, who instructed them to break through the city walls as quietly as possible. He then told the last escapees to walk backward to make their footprints unclear and confuse their pursuers. Their flight is celebrated on the first Saturday of November every year by the Anlo Ewe of the Volta region of Ghana in a festival known as Hogbetsotso Za. The festival brings together chiefs and commoners and is marked by lively, soul-stirring drumming and dancing.

FESTIVAL AND CEREMONY

MAJOR EVENTS IN WEST AFRICA

Performance and arts festival (Koudougou)	Burkina Faso
Festival Baia das Gatas	Cape Verde
Aboakyir Festival	Ghana
Panafest	Ghana
Homowo Festival	Ghana
Hogbetsotso Festival	Ghana
Bouake Carnival	Côte d'Ivoire
Festival of Masks	Côte d'Ivoire
Fête du Dipri	Côte d'Ivoire
Crossing of the cattle	Mali
Festival of Masks	Mali
Festival on the Niger	Mali
Durbar Festival	Nigeria

MANY DIFFERENT FESTIVALS ARE HELD THROUGHOUT THE YEAR IN WEST AFRICA, CELEBRATING VARIOUS ASPECTS OF LIFE. THE ARRAY OF EVENTS RANGES FROM TRADITIONAL CELEBRATIONS COMMEMORATING RITES OF PASSAGE, TO FESTIVALS OF CONTEMPORARY CULTURE.

TRADITIONAL FESTIVALS

Ghana has an especially rich heritage of traditional festivals involving music and dance. For example, dance-drumming festivals such as Godigbeza and Hogbetsotso are held by different branches of the Ewe people to commemorate their migration to safety from tyrannical rule in Togo in the 1600s (see EWE).

THE DARAL FESTIVAL OF THE FULANI

The Cattle Crossing, or Daral, at Diafarabé takes place every year in the Macina region of Mali. The Fulani lead their cattle here from the northern Sahel grazing grounds to cross the Niger river—narrow at this point—and wait for the return of the rains in May or June. As well as having this practical purpose, the Daral is a key social event, giving friends and family dispersed by seasonal pasturing a chance to meet up again. Music and dancing also form part of the celebrations.

In Ghana there are also many assemblies (*durbars*) convened by tribal chiefs. At these ceremonies, community leaders and Queen Mothers are paraded on decorated stretchers known as palanquins, shaded by parasols. The rulers wear their most lavish gold jewelry, and the processions are often accompanied by drummers and warriors firing ancient muskets.

The Asante of Ghana hold an occasional but very important durbar known as Adae Kese. This ceremony takes place in the Asante capital of Kumasi and attracts large numbers of both prominent and ordinary people. It marks particular milestones and significant achievements of the Asante kingdom. Adae Kese was originally held to celebrate the decisive military campaigns that the first *asantehene* (ruler) Osei Tutu waged against the neighboring Denkyera people between 1697 and 1699; these laid the foundations of the Asante kingdom. The festival is in two phases. In the first, the royal family and other chiefs from around the region perform solemn, private rituals at the king's palace chambers; there, the ancestral stools that symbolize kingship, including the most sacred and revered

At InGall in Niger, both the Tuareg (shown here) and Fulani peoples gather annually to celebrate a homecoming festival. They travel north to this place with their camels and cattle.

Golden Stool (*Sika 'dwa*), are purified. The second phase is a public durbar. This involves a colorful parade of Asante royalty, which provides the ordinary people with an opportunity to demonstrate their loyalty to their monarch. The Golden Stool, which is hardly ever shown in public, is displayed at these durbars. The most recent Adae Kese took place in May 2004, the first since 1991. This rare festival is vitally important to the Asante because it reinforces their strong sense of independence and history.

Among agriculturally based peoples, several festivals are associated with the annual harvest. A major celebration of this type is the yam harvest thanksgiving festival known as Odwira, in which the Akan cleanse themselves spiritually and get in touch with their dead ancestors to ask for guidance and protection. Another is the Homowo festival of the Ga. Literally meaning "making fun of hunger," it recalls a devastating famine that swept across the plains near Accra where the Ga people live. When the rains came and people could finally harvest they celebrated this with

Festivals that focus on cattle are central to livestock-herding cultures such as the Fulani. After eight months spent on the pastures of the northern Sahel, Fulani herders bring their cattle to cross the Niger River and celebrate the Daral festival.

a festival. *Oguua Fetu Afahye*, a harvest celebration held in Cape Coast, Ghana, combines thanksgiving for good fortune with a *durbar*. For cattle-herding peoples such as the Fulani, the most important festivals are those associated with livestock (see box feature; FULANI).

MODERN FESTIVALS

Other West African cultural festivals are of more recent origin. A large two-yearly festival called Panafest has been established in Ghana to celebrate Pan-African identity. It attracts people with Ghanaian roots from all over the world and incorporates traditional ceremonies such as initiations, music and dance performances, and dramatic events. Linked to Panafest, but celebrated even in the years when the main festival is not held, is Emancipation Day, commemorating the end of slavery. This was first observed in

THE ARGUNGU FISHING FESTIVAL

The Fishing and Cultural Festival at Argungu in northwestern Nigeria began in 1934 to mark the first visit there of the sultan of Sokoto, the ruler of a neighboring state with which Argungu had once been at war. Today it is a four-day cultural event held every January or February and attended by local and political dignitaries. The main event is a fishing contest, which takes place to the beat of drummers in canoes. Participants compete to catch the biggest fish in just one hour. In 2005, the winner, who takes home a brand-new bus and a million *naira* ($7,500), caught a fish weighing 165 pounds (75 kg).

1998, when the bodies of former Ghanaian slaves who had died in captivity abroad were brought home from Jamaica and the United States for burial. The ceremony proved so popular that it was decided to hold it annually.

Another festival with its origins in trans-atlantic slavery is the International Roots Festival in The Gambia, inspired by the African-American author Alex Haley's Pulitzer-prizewinning book *Roots* (1976). Haley traced his ancestry back to his forbear Kunta Kinte, who was enslaved and shipped to Maryland in 1767. A U.S. television miniseries based on the novel achieved phenomenal success. The festival was inaugurated in 1996 to enable people of the African diaspora to celebrate a homecoming and raise awareness of their heritage.

The Argungu Fishing and Cultural Festival (see box feature), which is held every year in February, was established to commemorate peace between the Fulani Sokoto caliphate and the Hausa Kebbi kingdom in the early 19th century.

Ségou in western Mali hosted the first Festival on the Niger in 2005; this lively cultural and arts festival is designed to celebrate the diverse mix of peoples in the country, and to showcase the music of Mali, which several artists have made famous worldwide. The Niger festival also includes dance, exhibitions, storytelling, and a craft fair and workshops.

THE OSHUN FESTIVAL

In the city of Oshogbo in southwestern Nigeria, the Yoruba hold a festival in August to honor Oshun, a water goddess who is associated with the river that flows through the town. Oshun is one of the most significant spirits (*orisha*; see AFRICAN RELIGIONS) in the Yoruba religion, and is believed to bring good fortune in love and marriage and to promote fertility among women. Celebrated in August, the festival allows people to make sacrificial offerings to Oshun—who is renowned for being generally benign and happy, but who is said to have a furious temper when angered.

The shrines to Oshun, situated in an area known as the Sacred Forest, had fallen into disuse by the late 1950s; however, they were restored thanks to the efforts of an Austrian sculptor, Suzanne Wenger (b.1915), who came to live in Oshogbo and became a follower of the Yoruba religion. Known as Adunni (adored one) to local people, Wenger helped revive the festival, which now draws many people to the region.

SEE ALSO: African religions; Akan; Dance and song; Ewe; Fulani; Islam; Masks and masquerade; Music and musical instruments; Yoruba.

The fast and furious excitement of the Argungu Fishing Festival in northern Nigeria. This event attracts some 2,500–3,000 contestants keen to win the valuable first prize. They are equipped with only a hand net and a hollowed-out gourd for their catch .

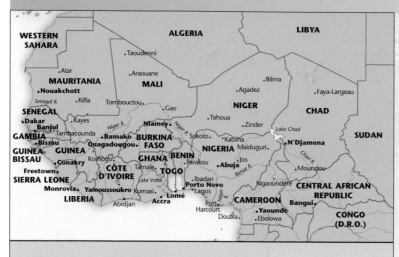

FACT FILE

Population	3.5 million (mostly in Benin; some in Togo)
Religion	Fon religion, Christianity, Islam
Language	The Fon language belongs to the Proto-Kwa branch of the Niger-Congo language family.

TIMELINE

1472	The Portuguese first explore the coast of the Gulf of Guinea.
early 1600s	Kingdom of Dahomey is founded at Abomey; it is a breakaway state from the Kingdom of Allada.
1700s–1800s	The coast of the Gulf of Guinea becomes known as the Slave Coast as hundreds depart as slaves from its shores.
1708–32	King Agaja of Dahomey conquers neighboring states of Allada and Whydah, gaining access to the coast and to Western traders selling firearms.
1807	The slave trade is abolished throughout the British empire.
1840s	As Britain enforces ban on overseas slave trade, Dahomey's fortunes (under King Gezu; 1818–58) wane.
1889–94	Dahomey is invaded by the French and later incorporated into French West Africa.
1960	Dahomey wins independence from France.
1963	The first president of Dahomey, Hubert Maga, is ousted in a military coup.
1972	Mathieu Kérékou comes to power.
1975	Dahomey is renamed the People's Republic of Benin.
1991	Multiparty elections are held and Nicéphore Soglo is elected president.
1996	Kérékou is reelected to power; January 10 declared a national holiday in honor of Vodun religion.

THE FON LIVE IN THE SOUTH OF THE SMALL STATE OF BENIN. IN FORMER TIMES, THE FON KINGDOM OF DAHOMEY WAS ONE OF WEST AFRICA'S MOST POWERFUL NATIONS.

HISTORY

The Fon kingdom of Dahomey (now within the modern country of Benin) was originally formed in the early 17th century as a breakaway state from the Kingdom of Allada. Its founder was a chief named Do-Aklin. Based around the capital of Abomey, it soon became one of the dominant powers in the region through aggressive military expansion. This process began under Do-Aklin's grandson Wegbaja (c.1645–85), but really came to a peak during the rule of King Agaja (r.1708–32). During these campaigns, the Fon earned themselves a reputation as fearless warriors. A bodyguard of around 2,500 female warriors was assigned to protect the king and hunt elephants. Throughout the 1700s and 1800s, Dahomey was often at war with other powerful kingdoms in the region, such as the Yoruba kingdoms of Oyo and Abeokuta. The Fon took an active part in the transatlantic slave trade (see box feature), supplying Europeans with war captives as slaves in exchange for firearms. Later, they dealt in palm oil, a major export commodity since the colonial era.

Despite fierce resistance, French colonial forces overran Dahomey in 1889–94.

SOCIETY AND DAILY LIFE

Most Fon live in villages and survive by farming, fishing, or market trading. Historically, the economy was based on agriculture, and this remains the case today. Farm labor is divided strictly along gender lines, with the men clearing and hoeing the

fields, while the women plant and harvest the crops. House building also involves gender-specific tasks; women prepare the wattle and daub (interwoven twigs and mud) to build the huts with, but adult men are responsible for the actual construction.

Fon society has always focused on the lineage, or extended family. The head of a lineage is the eldest male heir of a common ancestor, and the family live in adjoining compounds. However, this form of organization is gradually dying out as a result of the impact of modern life and other changes in the structure of society.

CULTURE AND RELIGION

The pre-Christian Fon religion involved the worship of several deities, or *vodun*. Although some Fon now follow Christianity or Islam, most still continue to worship the *vodun* and venerate their ancestors. Paying attention to and keeping the spirits content remains central to many of the cultural practices of the Fon.

A dancing kulito at a vodu festival in Porto Novo, Benin. The Fon believe that the kulito are the ghosts of ancestors, who come back to earth from time to time by possessing living people. As long as they are shown respect, these spirits help the community.

The Fon religion traveled to the New World during the era of slavery. There, it gave rise to what is sometimes called *voodoo*, often mistakenly linked to "black magic." Common features of voodoo include spirit possession and trances, rituals (such as animal sacrifices), and dancing. These activities are intended to appease certain spirits, which are not regarded as ill-willed but rather are believed to offer people advice and protection.

See also: African religions; Ewe; Masks and masquerade; Yoruba.

SLAVERY AND THE FON

At the height of the slave trade in the late 18th century, it is estimated that as many as 45,000 people a year were shipped from the coast of the Gulf of Guinea, with significant numbers coming from the region now known as Benin. The high number of slaves taken from this area is reflected in the way the religious practices of the Fon people have spread as far as Haiti in the Caribbean, where voodoo is now recognized as an official religion.

MAJOR WORKS AND THEIR AUTHORS

Title	Date	Author	Country
Anthologie de la Nouvelle Poésie Nègre et Malgache (New Anthology of Black and Malagasy Poetry)	1948	Léopold Senghor	Senegal
L'Enfant Noir (The Dark Child)	1954	Camara Laye	Guinea
Un Nègre à Paris (An African in Paris)	1959	Bernard Dadié	Côte d'Ivoire
Leurres et Lueurs (Lures and Glimmers)	1960	Birago Diop	Senegal
Les Bouts de Bois de Dieu (God's Bits of Wood)	1960	Birago Diop	Senegal
Le Revenant (The Ghost)	1976	Aminata Sow Fall	Senegal
Une si Longue Lettre (So Long a Letter)	1980	Mariama Bâ	Senegal
En Attendant le Vote des Bêtes Sauvages (Waiting for the Vote of the Wild Animals)	1998	Ahmadou Kourouma	Côte d'Ivoire
Riwan ou le Chemin sur le Sable (Riwan, or The Road on the Sand)	1999	Ken Bugul	Senegal

BECAUSE FRANCE TRIED TO PLAY DOWN LOCAL CULTURES IN ITS COLONIES, MANY ELOQUENT AND ORIGINAL AFRICAN WRITERS FIRST FOUND THEIR LITERARY VOICE IN FRENCH. MANY OF THEM USED THE LANGUAGE OF THEIR COLONIAL MASTERS TO EXPRESS CRITICISM AND CALL FOR CHANGE.

BEGINNINGS

In its African colonies, France operated a policy of assimilation—meaning that it imposed French cultural and social values on the people of its overseas possessions. The practical result of this policy was that the most gifted students from each colony were sent to Paris to complete their education and encouraged to think of themselves as French rather than African. It was in Paris in the 1930s that African and Caribbean writers began to write in French about their experiences of colonialism, and to voice their criticism of foreign rule.

EARLY THEMES

The early optimism that Francophone (French-speaking) Africans felt about the opportunities offered by assimilation soon gave way to disillusionment. Many West African intellectuals found it hard to reconcile their identity with the alien cultural values they were expected to adopt. The desire to reconnect with their African roots, and to reclaim their identity as educated Africans (rather than black Frenchmen), was central to the negritude (blackness) movement. This movement, which was given

The writers of the negritude movement condemned the damage that imperialism caused and the racist attitudes of European colonists. This scene from the 1967 play Une Saison au Congo, *by the playwright Aimé Césaire, shows the mistreatment of a political prisoner by white jailers.*

its name by the Caribbean writer Aimé Césaire from Martinique, asserted black pride and the struggle for recognition rather than assimilation.

FRENCH-LANGUAGE POETRY

One of the most famous and influential members of the negritude movement was the Senegalese poet Léopold Sédar Senghor (1906–2001), whose most famous works include *Chants d'ombre* (1945) and *Ethiopiques* (1956). Other influential poets in the movement include the Senegalese writers David Diop (1927–60), author of the book of poems *Coups de Pilon* (Hammer Blows 1956) and Birago Diop (1906–89), whose most famous work is the poetry collection *Leurres et Lueurs* (1960). He also wrote many folktales in the *griot* tradition.

Among the best-known contemporary poets are Frédéric Pacéré Titinga from Burkina Faso, who was awarded the 1982 *Grand Prix littéraire de l'Afrique noire* for his *Poèmes pour l'Angola* and *La Poésie des griots* and the poets Jacques Prosper Bazié and Bernadette Dao, also from Burkina Faso, both of whom have published many poetry collections.

FRENCH-LANGUAGE NOVELS

Through the diversity and richness of their work, African novelists have made a huge contribution to the body of literature written in French. Authors such as Ferdinand Oyono (b.1929) and Mongo Beti (1932–2001), both from Cameroon, wrote on themes such as colonial power relations, missionary activity, and identity. Many authors have been seen as dissidents in their home countries and their books banned. Camara Laye (1928–80), who was renowned for the psychological insights of his novels came into conflict with the authoritarian government of his native Guinea and fled to Senegal in 1965.

Although contemporary novels still treat the legacy of colonialism, they now focus

LÉOPOLD SÉDAR SENGHOR

The writer and statesman Léopold Sédar Senghor was a major influence on the development of the French-language literature of West Africa. Following a French-style education in Senegal and France, he became a teacher and later a politician in Paris. There he met like-minded black scholars and together they founded the journal *Présences Africaines* in 1947 to promote the negritude movement and publish the works of African authors. His edited collection of poems *Anthologie de la nouvelle poésie nègre et malgache* (1948) was the first work to introduce black writing from the French colonies to a wide international audience. He argued passionately for French colonies in Africa to be given their independence, and in 1960 was elected as the first President of Senegal. He retired in 1980—the first African president to leave office voluntarily—and died in France in 2001.

increasingly on other themes, such as women's rights, village life, or social change. The most famous French-language novelists include Sembène Ousmane (b.1923) who is also an internationally acclaimed film director, and the political satirist Ahmadou Kourouma (1927–2003) from Côte d'Ivoire, who won prizes for novels such as *Allah n'est pas obligé* (2000) and *En attendant le vote des bêtes sauvages* (1998). These two novels deal with the very topical issues of war, child soldiers, and political corruption in West Africa. Most writers are male, although some prominent female writers have also emerged, such as Aminata Sow Fall (b.1941), Mariama Bâ (1929–81), and Ken Bugul (b.1948). Short stories are also popular in West African literature; leading practitioners include the Ivorian Bernard Dadié (b.1916) and Birago Diop.

As well as being a highly respected man of letters, Léopold Senghor engaged himself in political life, both in France and in his native Senegal.

See also: African-language literature; English-language literature; Movies; Oral literature.

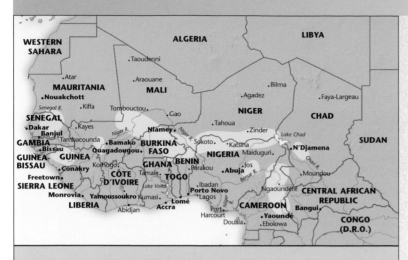

FACT FILE

Population	Nigeria 9,320,000; Guinea 3,800,000; Burkina Faso 1,718,000; Mali 1,700,000; Cameroon 1,600,000; Senegal 1,500,000; Niger 990,000; Benin 310,000; Gambia 286,000; Guinea-Bissau 245,000; Sierra Leone 166,000; Central African Republic 156,000
Religion	Islam
Language	The language of the Fulani, Fula, is a member of the Niger-Congo language family. It has nine dialects, including Fulfulde (from Mali to Cameroon, with different subgroups), Pular (Guinea), and Pulaar (Senegal; includes the Tukulor dialect).

TIMELINE

8th–13th centuries	Fulani migrate southward and eastward from present-day Senegal (or possibly farther north).
11th–13th centuries	Fulani adopt Islam and help spread the faith in the region.
1670s–1800	Fulani wage jihads against neighboring peoples. States of Futa Djallon, Futa Toro, Wuli, and Budu established.
1804–19	Usman dan Fodio elected Commander of the Believers, Fulani leaders found two Islamic empires: the Sokoto caliphate (Nigeria) and Macina empire (Mali).
1854–62	Tukulor leader Umar Tal conquers Macina; he aims to create a large empire to halt French invasion.
1897	Expanding eastward from Dakar (modern Senegal), the French take over the Tukulor empire.
1903	The armies of the Sokoto caliphate are defeated and the region annexed to the British colony of Nigeria.
1970s–1980	Droughts reduce Fulani herds, and drive the nomadic Fulani to compete with each other and more settled farmers. Many opt for a settled life or migrate to cities.
1980s–1990s	Fulani militants stage armed uprisings in Sahel region.

THE FULANI PEOPLE ARE WIDELY DISPERSED ACROSS WEST AFRICA. THIS IS MAINLY DUE TO THE NOMADIC LIFE OF CATTLE HERDING THAT THEY ALL ONCE LED. IN MODERN TIMES, BECAUSE THEY HAVE LOST THEIR HERDS TO DISEASE OR DROUGHT, OR BEEN FORCED BY POLITICAL PRESSURE, MANY FULANI HAVE SETTLED AND BECOME CROP-GROWING FARMERS.

HISTORY

The exact origins of the Fulani—also called the Fulbe, or Peul in French—are unknown and the subject of much debate. They are thought to have originated in the area of present-day Senegal or even farther north, from where they spread throughout West Africa from around 700 onward. Converting early to Islam, they played a key role in its spread, perhaps from as early as 1300. From the 17th to the 19th centuries, Fulani leaders waged jihads in the region. These reforming campaigns of holy struggle were undertaken to topple harsh rulers and establish fairer government.

The Fulani established a number of Islamic emirates in the Sahel (the southern fringes of the Sahara desert), of which the best-known are the Sokoto caliphate and the Macina empire. The Sokoto caliphate was the outcome of a campaign by Fulani cleric Usman dan Fodio (1754–1816), from the northern Hausa state of Gobir in modern Niger, to reform Hausa society. He won much support from the Hausa peasantry, who resented the heavy taxes that their oppressive rulers imposed and were ready to rise up against them. The jihad he sparked lasted from 1804 to 1809 and swept across Nigeria, stopping only at the borders of the Kanem-Bornu empire to the east.

Farther west, the Macina empire was founded by Sekou Amadou (1775–1844) in around 1819–21. Its capital Hamdallahi was located on the Inner Niger Delta in Mali. This city, which was protected by a brick wall over 3 miles (4.8 km) long, remains a place of pilgrimage today and a symbol of the strength of Islam.

The Tukulor, who live mainly in modern Senegal, are related to the Fulani. They

THE GEREWOL

The Gerewol, or Cure Salée, is an important festival held near the town of InGall in western Niger. Every year around September the Bororo Fulani and the Tuareg bring their cattle there to feed on the rich grazing land that is available when the salt flats flood. The occasion is also marked by camel races, dancing, and a beauty contest for bachelors, in which attractive men are chosen by girls to be their husbands. In modern times, the Gerewol has also become a forum for speeches by political leaders.

The Fulani Gerewol festival near InGall, Niger, involves a male beauty pageant. Men paint their faces with red ocher and other pigments, put on jewelry, and wear elaborate headdresses.

speak a dialect of Fulfulde but tend to be settled farmers rather than nomadic pastoralists. They also played a key role in spreading Islam. In the period 1854–62 their leader al-Hajj Umar (or Umar Tal; c.1797–1864) founded the Islamic Tukulor empire between the upper Senegal and Niger rivers as a successor state to Macina.

Between 1860 and 1915, all these Fulani states were conquered by relatively small French and British armies, which had the advantage of the latest military technology, such as field artillery and machine-guns.

SOCIETY AND DAILY LIFE

The Fulani who still pursue a seminomadic lifestyle, most notably the Bororo of Niger, typically occupy the northern Sahel, where inadequate rainfall prevents crop growing. Their main economic activity is raising long-horned zebu cattle, although sheep, camel, and goats are also kept. They occasionally trade live animals, meat, and dairy products with their agriculturalist neighbors. The Bororo move on a seasonal basis, allowing them to avoid water shortages, seek out fresh pasture for the herds, avoid disease, and make wide-ranging social and economic contacts. Characteristic of a people on the move, their dwellings are small and easy to transport, and their material possessions are kept to a bare minimum. The Wodaabe are a related group in northeastern Niger, numbering around 500,000, who are also cattle herders.

The typical household involves a herd owner, his wife or wives, and their children. The sons assist the father in herding, while the daughters help their mother with milking and making butter and cheese. Meat is only eaten on special

A Wodaabe Fulani man sporting a traditional raffia hat. These hats not only provide the wearer with protection against the sun, but also act as indicators of wealth and status. They may be decorated with leather and with cowrie shells.

FULANI HATS

The conical, colorful hats worn by men are a trademark of the Fulani. Made of woven raffia and (usually black and red) leather, they are typically topped with a prominent button; many Bororo Fulani add ostrich feathers to their hat. A thriving on-line market testifies to the popularity of these handmade items, for use either as protection against the sun or as wall decorations.

occasions, and animals are only sold when money is needed. Fulani proverbs, tales, myths, and songs largely revolve around the cattle that are central to this pastoral society. A Fulani measures his wealth and success by the number of cattle he owns, although among some it is impolite to mention the exact number of cows a person owns.

The nomadic life has been abandoned by large numbers of Fulani, either encouraged or forced by government programs to switch to a settled lifestyle, or driven to give up herding by the severe droughts that affected the region in the late 20th century. The Tukulor have been settled farmers and fishers for centuries; some people consider the Tukulor a separate ethnic group. A well-known member of this group is the musician Baaba Maal (b.1954), who sings in Pulaar.

CULTURE AND RELIGION

The Fulani are mainly Muslim, although they integrate this with a range of practices connected with spirit possession and magic, including beliefs relating to cattle.

Fulani artistic expression generally focuses on decorating the body or objects for everyday use. Fulani women are responsible for erecting the family tents or shelters and weaving wall and floor mats. They also decorate calabashes—a kind of large gourd— and wooden bowls using a technique of engraving with sticks heated in a fire. Milk bowls, which are symbolic of the pastoral life and of the cooperation between men and women, are a key emblem of Fulani identity. Above all, Fulani people are known for their mastery of the verbal arts, expressed through their songs and poetry.

The Fulani often entrust members of specialized castes or outsiders with the manufacture of more permanent objects such as jewelry. In the past, Fulani women wore gold and copper earrings, anklets, or necklaces, some of which may have once served as currency. Yet, as everywhere else,

Many Fulani, such as this Wodaabe woman in central Niger, are still seminomadic pastoralists who herd their cattle seasonally to different grazing lands. In tune with this lifestyle, their homes are tents or temporary raffia shelters woven by the women.

these fashions are losing ground to more modern materials; in addition, the impoverishment of many Fulani following the droughts of the 1970s and 1980s forced many women to part with their jewelry.

SEE ALSO: *Architecture; Festival and ceremony; Hausa; Islam; Oral literature; Textiles.*

HAMPÂTÉ BA

Amadou Hampâté Ba (1901–91), a Fulani from Bandiagara in Mali, was a man of many parts. He described himself variously as a poet, linguistic historian, anthropologist, theologian, religious mystic, Muslim, and a storyteller–comedian. He won fame far beyond the region for his passionate commitment to preserving and documenting the oral traditions of West Africa before they disappeared, through his work at the Institut Francophone d'Afrique Noire and UNESCO, the U.N. cultural organization. Of the richness of oral history, he said "In Africa, when an old person dies, it's like a library going up in flames." He wrote extensively on West African traditions, and two volumes of his memoirs, *Amkoullel l'enfant peul* (2000) and *Oui mon commandant* (2001), were published after his death.

ONE OF THE WAYS IN WHICH WEST AFRICAN PEOPLES MARK A PERSON'S DEATH IS BY MAKING SPECIAL OBJECTS, EITHER FOR USE AT THE FUNERAL OR TO HELP MAINTAIN CONTACT BETWEEN THE DEAD AND THE LIVING. ALTHOUGH ISLAM AND CHRISTIANITY HAVE ALTERED SUCH PRACTICES, THEY CONTINUE TO THRIVE AND EVOLVE IN MANY PLACES. THE COFFINS OF THE GA PEOPLE OF GHANA HAVE BECOME PARTICULARLY FAMOUS.

ANCESTOR FIGURES

In the past, the Oron people of southeastern Nigeria used to carve figures known as *ekpu* from pieces of hardwood whenever an elder of the village died. These carvings were then placed inside the men's meeting house, and were offered sacrifices of food and drink to preserve the well-being of the community and to ward off misfortune. Collectively, these figures also came to symbolize the lineages (that is, the shared ancestry) and rights of their descendants and so served to strengthen the authority of the surviving elders.

In the early 20th century, as Christian missionaries began to spread the Gospel in the region, many *ekpu* were neglected as the Oron religion declined. To try to preserve them, a museum was established locally (the Oron elders refused to let the carvings be moved from their place of origin). However, most of the carvings that were gathered and housed in the museum were stolen or destroyed in the Biafran War that raged in that part of Nigeria from 1967 to 1970. Moreover, the very act of placing them in a museum had robbed them of their original spiritual significance.

In the period following the Biafran War, the *ekpu* have taken on a new significance as powerful symbols of the cultural identity of the Oron people, and surviving examples can once more be seen on display in their original locality.

Carpenters from Teshie, Ghana, carry an elaborate coffin for the funeral of a fisher. Fantasy coffins do not just relate to professions—others are made in the shape of cellphones or soda cans.

GA FANTASY COFFINS

Many of the traditions of sculpture and carving in West Africa have fallen into neglect because of the rise of Christianity and the decline of preexisting beliefs. However, the Ga people who live near Accra in southern Ghana have bucked this trend by creating a whole new art form—ornate "fantasy" coffins. This industry, which has its center in the town of Teshie, developed when many local craftsmen who had learned carpentry during the economic boom of World War II (1939–45) and the immediate post-independence era began to apply their skills to funerary art. A prosperous new middle class provided a ready market for their extraordinary creations. The coffins symbolize the dead person's profession—fish for fishers, huge cigarettes for tobacconists, giant sewing machines for seamstresses, limousines for drivers, and so on. Not all are considered appropriate to be taken into church, and in such instances may only be permitted access to the churchyard. So famous have Teshie's fantasy coffins become that the makers no longer supply just their local market; their works have featured in several major exhibitions in museums around the world and have been bought by Western art galleries.

inspired by European paintings and prints—Kalabari culture was very open to influences from other societies. Amachree I may well have encouraged their introduction after being denied access to traditional Kalabari objects of power because of his humble background. Each screen shows a particular ancestor dressed in the ceremonial outfit he would have worn when still alive. Although in reality this ceremonial garb would have included a mask, on the screens their faces are bare. The screens were kept in the headquarters of the trading houses, where the spirits of the dead were thought to return every eight days to receive offerings and hear the latest news. Today, Christian Kalabari people may appoint a non-Christian deputy to perform such rituals. The modern steel sculptures of performing masked figures made by the Kalabari woman artist Sokari Douglas Camp (b.1958) have strong echoes of the funerary screens.

TERRACOTTA FIGURINES

In other parts of West Africa clay is the main medium for funerary art. For example, the Akan peoples of coastal Ghana and Côte d'Ivoire have a tradition, going back at least to the 16th century, of creating terracotta sculptures of the head of the dead person. These range from small, solid clay heads to hollow ones that are almost life-size. Special attention is paid to reproducing every detail of facial scarification and hairstyle. Some were left unpainted while others were colored. Female artists made such sculptures to honor dead chiefs and elders, and portrayed not only the deceased but also his family and courtiers. The statues were kept in a sacred grove near the cemetery, where food, drink, and prayers were offered up to them. These shrines were known as *mmaso*, and in some areas the practice continued up to the 1970s.

SEE ALSO: African religions; Akan; Festival and ceremony; Masks and masquerade; Sculpture.

KALABARI FUNERARY SCREENS

From the late 15th century the Kalabari people of the Niger delta were important middlemen in trade between Africa, Europe, and the Americas. Trade was controlled by rival trading houses, some of which came to be led by individuals with slave origins. One such person was Amachree I (c.1600–66), who was the first ex-slave to become king and the first to be commemorated by a carved wooden funerary screen. These carved screens are thought to have been

A Kalabari funerary screen depicting an ancestral house-head wearing the masquerade outfit that he wore when living. Shown on the head of the figure is a full-rigged sailing ship, representing the wealth that the community acquired from Western trade.

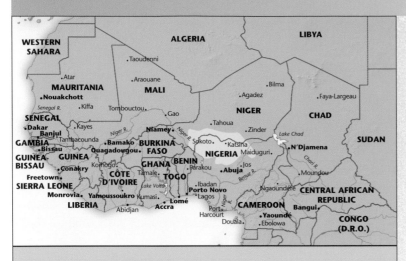

FACT FILE

Population	Nigeria 20,000,000; Niger 6,500,000; Sudan 490,000
Religion	Islam
Language	Hausa, one of the principal languages of West Africa, is part of the Afro-Asiatic family. Up to another 15,000,000 people are thought to speak Hausa as a second language in West Africa.

TIMELINE

999	City of Kano founded, according to the *Kano Chronicle*.
1380s	According to the *Kano Chronicle* the Wangara arrive in Kano and Muslim prayer is held throughout the land.
15th century	The Hausa are mentioned for the first time by the Egyptian historian al-Maqrizi, who calls them Afnu. They have extensive links with neighboring Kanem-Borno, Songhai, and Aïr.
16th century	The European authors Leo Africanus and Giovanni d'Anania describe the rich and civil merchants of Kano and Zaria.
1804–17	A Fulani jihad led by Usman dan Fodio brings the creation of the Sokoto caliphate. Fulani replace the traditional Hausa rulers.
1895–1915	The Hausa area falls under the control of the British and the French.
1960	Nigeria and Niger attain independence.
1975	Capital of Nigeria moved from Lagos to Abuja.
1980–82	More than 4,000 people die in rioting by a fringe Islamic cult under the leadership of Maitatsine in Kano.
2000	Islamic Sharia law is instituted in Kano province, Nigeria.
2002	One hundred people die in clashes in Lagos, Nigeria, between Hausa from the Islamic north of the country and Yoruba from the Christian south.

THE HAUSA ARE THE LARGEST ETHNIC GROUP IN WEST AFRICA. THEY HAVE LONG EXERTED A GREAT INFLUENCE THROUGHOUT THE REGION BECAUSE OF THEIR INVOLVEMENT IN CLOTH MANUFACTURE AND TRADING. THE HAUSA HEARTLAND IN NORTHERN NIGERIA AND SOUTHERN NIGER CENTERS ON A NUMBER OF CITIES— ZARIA, KATSINA, KANO, GOBIR, AND DAURA—EACH WITH ITS OWN DISTINCTIVE ATMOSPHERE.

HISTORY

The Sahara, Lake Chad, and the present-day Hausa heartland have all been suggested as the place where the first Hausa settlements grew up, probably around 1,000 years ago. Hausa society is thought to have come into being as a result of small communities— typically a few houses and fields surrounded by a stockade—gradually amalgamating to form larger political and social units.

What is certain is that by 1600 the Hausa had established a series of city-states with wide-ranging trade contacts and industries. These cities were defended by impressive mud walls up to 60 feet (18 m) high. Early Western travelers reported Kano to be a bustling city. The Hausa city-states vied with one another to gain economic predominance. Archaeologists investigating such cities as Kargi, Kufan Kanawa, Maleh, Santolo-Fangwai, and Zaria have found that they covered a large area and had economies based on agriculture and long-distance trade. Over time, the city-states divided production and labor between them according to location and resources: Katsina and Daura, for example, became known as "Chiefs of the Market," thanks to their location at the end of trans-Saharan caravan routes.

The European colonial powers were well aware of the economic potential of the Hausa city-states and were keen to gain control of the region. In 1900, Kano was renowned as the great meeting-point of the central Sahel (the southern fringes of the Sahara), with industries and trade so extensive that more than half the region's people were clothed from there. Within a decade the Hausa area had been overrun and divided up between the French and British governments. Arbitrary state frontiers drawn by the colonial administrations divided the Hausa and are still in force today.

Niger and Nigeria achieved independence in 1960 (from France and Britain, respectively), and the Hausa are active on the modern political scene, particularly in Nigeria. Above all, Hausa "big men" still enjoy a reputation as skilled traders.

SOCIETY AND DAILY LIFE

Historically the Hausa were agriculturists (crop growers), who cultivated millet and sorghum. Most Hausa still work on the land, and as well as growing crops now also often own cattle, which are entrusted to local Fulani herders for rearing (the herder keeps the cows' milk as payment). Other, seasonal, activities are of great importance, particularly during the long, dry season between October and April in northern Nigeria and southern Niger, when no farming can be undertaken. Foremost among these activities are craft manufacture and trading.

In some Hausa communities, particularly urban centers in Nigeria, the seclusion of women is increasingly practiced in keeping with Islamic custom. Women remain within

In the city of Kano, the center of the Hausa lands, a festival known as Hawan Daushe is held every year at the end of the Islamic holy month of Ramadan. During this durbar ceremony, colorfully garbed noblemen and 50,000 soldiers on decorated horses pay homage to the emir, the region's ruler.

the walls of their compounds; errands, as well as small businesses such as the selling of kola nuts or millet pancakes, are delegated to or run by the children of the household.

CULTURE AND RELIGION

It is known that the first Hausa people practiced their own form of religion based around spirit worship. Mande traders and missionaries from the west are thought to have brought Islam to Kano and Katsina in around the 14th century. Islamic influence may also have come from the eastern state of Kanem-Borno, whose rulers converted to Islam as early as the 11th century. The number of converts to Islam was probably small at first, with preexisting religious beliefs being practiced alongside the new faith.

Over time, Islam came to play an ever greater role in society, and by the 15th century the Hausa cities were firmly linked to the wider Islamic world. North African writers reported on the Hausa for the first time; the scholar and cleric Al-Maghili came to advise Hausa rulers on proper Islamic practice; learned men settled in places such as Kano, and books became

Molded relief designs surround a window of a house in the Hausa region of Nigeria. Recent variants of this traditional art form may incorporate modern motifs, such as cars, in the design.

DECORATED HOUSES IN ZINDER

Zinder in southern Niger has many striking examples of traditional Hausa mud-plaster architecture. All around the sultan's palace from the time of the Sokoto caliphate, and in the neighborhood where trans-Saharan traders once halted, are mud-brick houses that stay cool in hot weather. These are decorated with a variety of designs, many of which are repeated from other forms of Hausa art, such as embroidered tunics. The traditional technique uses *makuba*, clay mixed with the oil of the locust-bean tree to make it more durable. Modern artisans use cement and commercial colorants, and even embed colored enamelware into their designs.

more common. The Hausa lands changed drastically after 1800, as the jihads undertaken by the Fulani swept across West Africa. The Sokoto caliphate was founded in the northern part of modern Nigeria (most of the Hausa cities of Niger remained independent) and Fulani rulers replaced the Hausa kings.

Today, most Hausa are Muslim. The major Hausa festivals are based on the Muslim calendar. They are an opportunity for Hausa hereditary rulers, who still wield power alongside modern government politicians, to assert their status and to parade in their finery with their attendants. Some "spirit cults" of the Hausa, such as the Maguzawa, blend worship of spirits called *bori* with Islam.

Hausa craftspeople are especially known for their leatherwork, indigo dyeing, embroidery, and metalwork. A characteristic Hausa architectural tradition is to decorate the façades of houses with mud and cement patterns in relief (see box feature).

SEE ALSO: *African religions; African-language literature; Fulani; Islam; Leatherwork; Oral literature; Yoruba.*

One of the seven true city-states of the Hausa, Kano grew prosperous in the Middle Ages from the trans-Saharan trade in salt, ivory, gold, and slaves. It also became famous at that time for exporting soft red "Morocco" leather.

THE LEGEND OF KUSUGU WELL

Hausa oral histories tell of a prince from the east called Bayajida who arrived in the northern Hausa city of Daura (now in Katsina state, Nigeria) in around 1100 C.E. and promptly killed a snake that was preventing people from using the city's well. In gratitude the local queen married him, and their seven sons went on to rule the seven city-states of the Hausa.

Although Bayajida was likely a mythical figure, the legend has endured. The Kusugu well in Daura, which is identified with the story, is a popular attraction for visitors and its water is said to cure many ailments.

FACT FILE

Population	Nigeria 23,000,000
Religion	Igbo religion, Christianity
Language	Igbo belongs to the Niger-Congo language family. It covers a range of more or less mutually intelligible dialects. A standard literary form is developing based on two dialects, Owerri amd Umuahia.

TIMELINE

8th–11th centuries	Communities at Igbo-Ukwu participate in long-distance trade networks.
mid-15th century	Portuguese make the first contact with coastal Igbo; other European nations gradually gain in influence, and Igbo people are taken in great numbers as slaves to work in the Americas.
1807	Slavery banned in the British Empire; palm oil, timber, elephant tusks, and spices became major trade goods instead. Unofficially, slavery continues to thrive for some 50 years after abolition.
1897–1900	Britain conquers Nigeria and introduces a system of indirect rule through chiefs imposed on the Igbo.
1960	Nigeria gains independence from Britain.
1967–70	Biafran (Civil) War in Nigeria. Three southeastern Igbo states proclaim the independent state of Biafra. After three years of bloody civil war the Biafran Army is defeated and Nigeria reunified.
1974	Oil boom in Nigeria; most of the oil deposits are in the Niger Delta, in Igbo territory.
1999	Olusegun Obasanjo is elected president of Nigeria. One of the major challenges facing modern Nigeria is the integration of its hugely diverse ethnic groups.
2004	Violent clashes between rival groups in southern oil city of Port Harcourt leave hundreds dead.

T HE IGBO, SOMETIMES SPELLED IBO, LIVE IN SOUTHEASTERN NIGERIA AND ARE THE THIRD LARGEST ETHNIC GROUP IN THIS LARGE COUNTRY OF 250 DIFFERENT PEOPLES. THEIR ATTEMPT TO FOUND THEIR OWN STATE, BIAFRA, IN 1967 SPARKED A DEVASTATING CIVIL WAR.

HISTORY

The earliest evidence of Igbo culture comes from Igbo-Ukwu, where archaeological excavations uncovered several hundred ceremonial copper alloy and bronze objects (see METALWORK), along with textiles, ceramics, and tens of thousands of glass and carnelian beads, many of them probably of southern Asian manufacture. This evidence of craft specialists, wealth accumulation, and long-distance trade around 900 C.E. suggests that Igbo society was already enjoying a healthy agricultural surplus (mostly of yams or palm oil). However, hunting and fishing would still have played important roles in sustaining the community.

Oral history tells of waves of immigrants settling in the heart of the Igbo region between the 9th and 15th centuries and gradually being absorbed. Trade along the Niger River was already well developed by the time European traders arrived on the scene in the late 15th century. The following 350 years were marked by the transatlantic slave trade; a loose confederation under the leadership of an Igbo–Ibibio clan acted as one of the main exporters of slaves, who often came from other Igbo groups. Trade continued to thrive even after slavery was abolished through major Igbo commercial centers, such as Aboh, located along the Niger River.

As British interest in the area grew during the 19th century, the territory of the Igbo increasingly came to be treated as a colony.

Military conquest was completed in the early 20th century, and taxes were levied for the first time on Igbo men in 1928.

Nigerian independence was declared in October 1960. However, the British colonial system fueled hostilities among the diverse peoples of Nigeria, and conflicts soon broke out in the independent Nigeria. The most bloody clash of all came in 1967 when the Igbo broke away from the Nigerian state to found the independent republic of Biafra. The resulting civil war that crushed the rebel state lasted for three years and caused 1 million casualties.

Since 1998, democratically elected rulers have ruled Nigeria. It has the potential to be a wealthy country, given its large reserves of oil. Yet many of these deposits lie within Igbo territory and are claimed by the Igbo, who resent the dominance in government of their northern Muslim neighbors the Hausa-Fulani.

SOCIETY AND DAILY LIFE

The village economy of the Igbo society is primarily based on farming, with special emphasis given to growing the yam as a symbol of prosperity and success. In the past, it was customary to ask a prospective son-in-law how big his yam barn was in order to gauge his wealth.

The social structure and government of different Igbo groups vary in detail from place to place, but are generally democratic. Living in small settlements, the Igbo mostly

A 19th-century clay shrine crafted to celebrate the yearly Ikeji new yam harvest festival. The figures represent a male chief (center) flanked by two pregnant wives, symbolizing fertility.

have no hereditary chiefs (except in the far north and west of Igbo territory), but instead invest authority in individuals who are distinguished by their ability or experience. These people are chosen by popular assent. The basic unit of Igbo society has historically been the village group, and the family head, usually the eldest man, was responsible for settling family disputes and communicating with the ancestors.

CULTURE AND RELIGION

The most important Igbo ceremony is the Ikeji (New Yam) festival, which is celebrated annually between August and October. It is an occasion to thank the ancestors for a productive year and to pray for good future harvests. Festivities begin with the eldest man in the community solemnly eating the season's first yams. Dancing, feasting, and masquerades then take place. Ikeji is also celebrated by Igbo living abroad.

The masks used in masquerades symbolize individual spirits, and signify the spirits' approval of the ceremonies. Uninitiated members of the group are forbidden from witnessing masquerades, and are expected to run away from them or risk being cursed.

SEE ALSO: *English-language literature; Hausa; Masks and masquerade; Metalwork; Yoruba.*

CHINUA ACHEBE

Albert Chinualumogu Achebe, born in 1930 to evangelical Igbo parents, is considered by many to be one of the best novelists now writing in the English language. His first novel, *Things Fall Apart,* appeared in 1958 and has been translated into some 50 languages. Achebe's satire, keen ear for dialog, and description of the effects of Western customs on African society explain his enduring popularity.

TIMELINE

622 C.E.	The Prophet Muhammad sets up a community in Medina; this hijra, or withdrawal, marks the beginning of the Muslim calendar.
mid–late 7th century	Islam spreads to most of North Africa.
10th–12th centuries	Rulers throughout the Sahel convert to Islam.
13th–17th centuries	Missionary activity flourishes among West Africans; the Fulani and Mande people are key in the process.
1804–62	Fulani Islamic leaders embark on holy wars (jihads) and found three important empires: the Sokoto caliphate (Nigeria), the Tukulor caliphate (Senegal), and the Macina empire (Mali).
late 19th century	Islam gains increasing popularity among commoners in West Africa.
2000–01	Six northern Nigerian states institute sharia law.

ISLAM SPREAD FROM ITS ARABIAN HEARTLAND THROUGH NORTH AFRICA IN THE LATE SEVENTH AND EARLY 8TH CENTURY, AND BEGAN TO ESTABLISH ITSELF IN WEST AFRICA IN AROUND 1000. ARAB AND BERBER MERCHANTS BROUGHT THE NEW FAITH ACROSS THE SAHARA DESERT. AS A RESULT, IT WAS AMONG THE PEOPLES OF THE SAHEL—THE SOUTHERN FRINGE OF THE SAHARA—THAT ISLAM TOOK FIRMEST ROOT.

HISTORY

The particular form of Islam that trans-Saharan traders brought with them to West Africa was called Kharijism. Characterized by its democratic outlook, it was this variant that the Berbers of North Africa and the Sahara accepted in around 700, finding it well suited to their clan-based society.

Kharijite Muslims from the north had established trade links with the Sahel by the 10th century. Efforts at religious conversion focused first on the rulers of the peoples inhabiting this region. For example, the Sefawa dynasty that controlled the empire of Kanem-Borno around Lake Chad is known to have adopted Islam in the mid-11th century (see KANURI). Islam was restricted for some while to the elites, with most ordinary people continuing to follow their preexisting beliefs. However, over time, the new faith spread south and west and also penetrated down through the social hierarchy to reach the common people. In the 11th century, the Spanish-Arab

A young girl reads aloud from the Quran during instruction at an Islamic school in Nigeria. In the early 2000s, six provinces in northern Nigeria instituted Islamic law (sharia).

THE GREAT MOSQUE AT DJENNÉ

The Great Mosque at Djenné in Mali is built in the style known as Sudanic, referring to the origins of this architecture in the Muslim lands of the Western Sudan. The present mosque was rebuilt in 1907 on the site of one that had existed there from the 13th century onward; it can hold up to 5,000 worshippers. Like all Sudanic mosques, it is built of dried clay. It has three towers more than 30 ft (9 m) high, and the walls are supported by strong, integral pillars on the outside (called buttresses). Another characteristic feature is the use of *toron*—wooden beams protruding like the spines of a hedgehog from the building's towers and walls. These beams give the structure strength and are decorative, but are also used to position scaffolding on when the mosque has to be resurfaced with wet clay. Replastering has to take place every year, since wind erosion and rain damage take a heavy toll on the walls.

geographer Al-Bakri described Kumbi Saleh, capital of the Soninke empire of Ghana (in modern Mauritania) as having a Muslim population and no fewer than 12 mosques. By the following century, thousands of West

African Muslims were making the pilgrimage (hajj) to the holy city of Mecca in Arabia.

In the later medieval period, three Islamic empires dominated the Sahel: Kanem-Borno (11th–19th centuries), Mali (c.1240–1500) and its successor state of Songhai (c.1460–1590). Mali was a driving force in spreading Islam; traders from the Mande people who founded the Empire of Mali introduced the religion to the Hausa in the 14th century.

Idris Aloma, who ruled Kanem-Borno from 1570 to 1600, greatly expanded its territory eastward, overrunning the pagan Wadai and Bagirmi states.

In a village in western Mali, a mosque towers above the straw roofs of homes and granaries. Throughout the Sahel, mosques are characterized by their clay walls and protruding beams.

The late 18th century saw the creation of Islamic brotherhoods, or *tariqa*, founded by charismatic religious leaders. Some of the earliest and strongest of these were the Tijaniyya and Qadiriyya brotherhoods. Around the same time, there arose in Senegambia and beyond jihad movements dedicated to toppling harsh rulers and establishing fairer government through popular revolt. The Sokoto caliphate created by the Islamic reformer Usman dan Fodio and the Tukulor caliphate of al-Hajj Umar—which built on the earlier Macina empire of Sekou Amadou—were strong regional powers until their conquest by colonial forces at the end of the 19th century (see FULANI).

Today, Islam remains the major religious, social, and political force in the countries of the Sahel. All of the population of Mauritania is Muslim, 90 percent of Mali's, and 80 percent of Niger's. In total, 65 percent of all West Africans are Muslim.

The Mourides brotherhood is an influential Islamic order to which many people in present-day Senegal and Gambia belong. It was founded in 1883 by Cheikh Amadou Bamba (1850–1927), a spiritual leader (*marabout*) and devotee of Islamic mysticism (Sufism), who claimed that salvation could come through hard work. Bamba was exiled in 1898 by the French colonial authorities, who feared his power.

MARRIAGE AND FAMILY

All followers of Islam, including those in West Africa, act in accordance with certain key principles (known as the Five Pillars). These are: the profession of faith, daily prayer at five appointed times, fasting during Ramadan, the giving of alms, and pilgrimage to Mecca at least once in a person's lifetime.

Muslim family life is based on edicts laid down in the Quran—the word of God as revealed to His Prophet Muhammad by the Angel Jibril (Gabriel)—and on lessons taken from the life of the Prophet. The family unit consists of a man, his wife or wives (up to four are permissible), and their children.

Islam accords great importance to the well-being of Muslims everywhere, and so looks upon the global community (*ummah*) of Muslims as a worldwide family.

FESTIVALS AND CEREMONIES

Because the Muslim calendar is based on lunar months, the dates on which major Islamic festivals fall vary from year to year. A major festival is the holy month of Ramadan, during which no food or water is consumed from sunrise to sunset. Because fasting, and in particular drinking no water, is demanding in hot weather, people often alter their schedules to sleep through the hottest hours of the day and work during the cooler periods. This can mean rising at three in the morning for a light meal and work. At sunset, the end of the day's fast is announced, and food is eaten; in West Africa, this is often millet porridge. Later, a larger meal might be eaten, and people visit each other, and talk throughout the night. The end of Ramadan is marked by a major celebration, Eid ul-Fitr, at which people put on their finest clothes and local dignitaries take part in parades.

Another important festival, Eid ul-Adha, is widely known throughout West Africa as Tabaski (from the Wolof word meaning "sacrifice"). It commemorates the sacrifice Abraham was prepared to make when Allah asked him to kill his son Isaac, before Allah intervened at the last moment and substituted a sheep. Each family head kills a sheep, which is roasted and shared among neighbors, friends, family, and the poor.

SEE ALSO: *Architecture; Fulani; Hausa; Kanuri; Mande; Moors; Mossi; Songhai; Wolof.*

Every year, some 500,000 members of the Mourides Islamic Brotherhood make a pilgrimage (magal) to the city of Touba in Senegal. The mosque there, built over the tomb of Cheikh Amadou Bamba, is the largest in West Africa.

KANURI

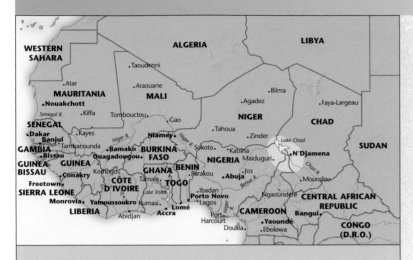

FACT FILE

Population	Nigeria 5,000,000; Niger 450,000; Chad 226,000; Cameroon 60,000
Religion	Islam
Language	Kanuri is part of the Nilo-Saharan language family and includes a range of dialects such as Kaga, Dagara, Kabari, and Mao.

TIMELINE

600–800	The founders of Kanem settle near Lake Chad.
c.1000	Kanem grows wealthy through the capture and export of slaves to North Africa. The Sefawa dynasty takes power in Kanem, and rules continuously for 850 years.
1060s	Kanem converts to Islam.
1200s	Kanem reaches the height of its power under Mai Dunama Dibalami, who commands a large cavalry force.
1400–1500	State becomes known as Kanem-Borno as power shifts to Borno and new capital of Ngarzagamu is built.
c.1571–1603	Idris III Aloma makes Kanem-Borno the greatest state between the Niger and the Nile.
1804–09	Kanem-Borno weakened by the jihad of Fulani cleric Usman dan Fodio of the Sokoto caliphate.
1893	Rabeh, a Shuwa Arab slave trader from Darfur, overruns Borno. British defeat Rabeh and abolish slavery.
1905 onward	Kanuri come under French and British colonial rule.
1976	Borno state, embracing much of precolonial Borno, is created in Nigeria.

THE AREA IMMEDIATELY AROUND LAKE CHAD, SOUTH OF THE SAHARA DESERT, IS HOME TO THE KANURI (CALLED THE BERIBERI BY THE HAUSA, THEIR NEIGHBORS). SINCE THE BORDERS OF FOUR COUNTRIES MEET IN THIS LARGE LAKE, KANURI COMMUNITIES EXIST NOT ONLY IN ALL THE MAJOR CITIES OF NORTHERN NIGERIA BUT ALSO IN NIGER AND, TO A LESSER EXTENT, IN CHAD AND CAMEROON.

HISTORY

The Kanuri are associated with one of the most important and long-lived African states—Kanem-Borno. Founded in the eighth century on the eastern shore of Lake Chad, this state eventually covered parts of Libya, Chad, Nigeria, Niger, and Cameroon. Its most famous ruler was Mai Dunama Dibalami (c.1210–59).

Kanem-Borno was in regular contact with North Africa from 1200 onward, playing a key role in trade and the spread of Islam. Over time, the center of the state shifted: Birni Gazargamu was the capital of the Bornu kingdom, while Kukawa was founded as the Kanuri capital in 1814.

It is unclear exactly when the Kanuri people and their language came into being, sometime between the 15th and 19th centuries. What is certain is that the Kanuri gradually came to dominate Kanem-Borno. Their rise to power was fiercely resisted by some groups, who were never fully absorbed; one key aspect of the Kanuri today is their great linguistic and cultural diversity.

SOCIETY AND DAILY LIFE

The Kanuri are settled farmers who rely on the hoe as their main tool for cultivating the land. Millet and sorghum (guinea corn),

made into dumplings or porridge and served with sauces, are the staple food crops. Groundnuts (peanuts) and cotton are grown for sale, while people who live on the shores of Lake Chad and along rivers such as the Yobe also fish. The Kanuri keep donkeys, sheep, and goats, and barter cattle from livestock herders such as the Fulani in exchange for grain and craft goods.

Before European contact, formal Kanuri society had a complex class structure made up of royal lineages, a land-owning nobility, peasants, and slaves. However, people living in small, agriculturally based communities were more or less equal in terms of wealth, and all belonged to the same social class.

Although the present political structure among the Kanuri is a product of the colonial era, its core social values date from precolonial times. Popular elections, new trading opportunities, and more widespread education have enabled common people to join the ranks of the leaders and of the wealthy, but traditional rulers still play an important role. Nigeria's Borno state consists of three emirates and four chiefdoms, whose leaders wield great political and religious authority.

CULTURE AND RELIGION

Kanuri society emphasizes the importance of the nuclear family and the authority of the father. Since the Kanuri have practiced Islam for nearly 1,000 years law, education, and social organization now show clear Muslim influence. Major festivals that are celebrated by the Kanuri include Ramadan and Tabaski (Eid ul-Adha).

SEE ALSO: Fulani; Hausa; Islam.

A Kanuri woman from the city of Maiduguri in northeastern Nigeria. In accordance with Islamic tradition, her head is covered with a veil for modesty.

KANURI JOKING RELATIONSHIPS

Most Kanuri see themselves not just as Kanuri, but also as members of one of the many subgroups. Between these groups there exist joking relationships, a common feature in many African societies. People in such relationships are not only permitted (or even required) to make gentle fun of each other, but are also expected to help each other out in times of need by donating food or money. Intermarriage among such groups is also encouraged, since the habit of joking helps lighten any quarrels that may arise between partners. In the Kanuri area, groups who have a joking relationship with one another are known as *ningima*.

LEATHERWORKING IS A THRIVING INDUSTRY IN MODERN WEST AFRICA. RELYING ON THE WIDESPREAD AVAILABILITY OF COWHIDES AND SHEEPSKINS IN AN AREA WHERE LIVESTOCK HERDING IS A MAINSTAY OF THE ECONOMY, LEATHERWORKING CAN BE TRACED FAR BACK INTO THE REGION'S PAST.

TRADITIONAL LEATHERCRAFT

The earliest evidence of leatherworking in West Africa comes from ancient rock art in the southern Sahara. These drawings show men clothed in tunics, which archaeologists believe may have been made of leather. This supposition was supported by the later discovery of 4,000-year-old scraps of leather in nearby tombs.

From the 15th century on, leather goods were among West Africa's most famous exports. They were bartered with North African merchants from across the Sahara in exchange for Middle Eastern cotton and muslin fabrics, weapons and metalwork from Europe, and North African wool. Some parts of West Africa—notably the Hausa areas—became fully geared to the production and export of leather, for which they enjoyed an extensive market. Tripoli, in Libya, developed into a distribution center for prized leatherwork from the Hausa cities. In Western Europe, the supple, deep red leather produced in Kano and the surrounding region went by the misleading name of "Morocco leather."

Leatherworking was traditionally an exclusively male occupation, and was often the preserve of a specialist group, or caste. This was the case among the Mande and the Wolof. Skins of both large livestock (cows) and small animals (sheep, goats) were used. The hides were treated (tanned) with natural plant extracts to loosen the flesh from the skins, and to make the leather supple through repeated soaking. These methods are increasingly being replaced by industrial tanning processes.

Today West African leatherwork is principally focused on the tourist trade. Leatherworkers often organize themselves into syndicates, each with their own separate outlets in the craft markets of West African capitals. This lively sector is quick to respond to changing consumer demands. Briefcases, poufs (large floor cushions), bags with stitched or appliquéd designs, wallets, and embossed photo frames are among the many items they produce.

Many of the precolonial states of the Sahel region were known for their formidable cavalry forces. Leather was used to make the bridles and other tack for these mounted units. This horse harness (above), inset with copper and bronze, comes from the Kanem-Borno empire.

HAUSA *TANDU*

Tandu was a technique used by Hausa craftsmen from Nigeria in precolonial times, involving molding thin pieces of cowhide over a clay core to make objects of a particular shape. Typically, small flasks were turned out, which were then decorated with strips of dyed leatherwork. Finally, leather loops, flaps, and fringes were sewn onto them. Closed with small cork stoppers, these flasks were used to store substances such as antimony (a silvery-white metal), which was applied as eye make-up. These *tandu* flasks could be bought at markets as far distant from their place of manufacture as Sudan and Algeria.

FUTURE PROSPECTS

Leatherwork has been identified as one of the key areas of potential growth for African economies. Already leather goods from Africa in the form of handbags, wallets, and shoes have benefited from tariff reductions introduced by the United States' African Growth and Opportunity Act (AGOA) of 2000. In the long term, the industry may prove invaluable to West Africa's prosperity: early in 2003, the value of the world market in leather was estimated at over $50 billion.

This figure greatly exceeds the value of commodities such as coffee or rice. Africa as a whole is estimated to have one-quarter of the world's sheep, so the commercial potential of leather is clear. However, the development of a shoe industry in West Africa is being hindered by cheap imports from other parts of the world, notably China, and the influx of second-hand goods from industrialized nations.

SEE ALSO: *Hausa; Kanuri; Mande; Wolof.*

Although most leatherworking in West Africa is now an industrial process, traditional skills are still employed. This leatherworker from Agadez, Niger, is removing hair from a soaked hide.

MANDE

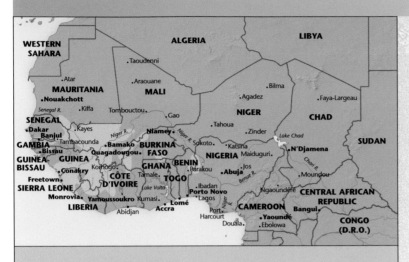

FACT FILE

Population Mali 6,200,000; Guinea 4,700,000; Côte d'Ivoire 4,500,000; Sierra Leone 2,600,000; Liberia 1,270,000; Burkina Faso 1,225,000; Senegal 1,205,000; Gambia 670,000; Ghana 181,000; Guinea-Bissau 160,000; Nigeria 99,000; Benin 71,000; Mauritania: 30,000

Religion Mande religion, Islam

Language 71 Mande languages (Niger-Congo family) are spoken in western West Africa. Bamana, from the Manding subgroup, is Mali's largest single language.

TIMELINE

5th–11th centuries Clans of the Soninke people come together and found ancient Ghana, linking the North African coast and the gold mines of West Africa through trade.

13th century The Mali empire rises under the rule of Sundiata Keita.

13th–14th centuries The fortunes of Mali wax and wane. Sundiata Keita transforms Timbuktu into a focus for trade and scholarship. Mali's influence is thought to extend to the Atlantic coast and down the Niger River to Gao.

15th century A combination of weak and ineffective rulers and increasingly aggressive raids by Mossi neighbors and Tuareg Berbers gradually reduces the power of Mali. In the 15th century only a small part of its former territory still exists. By 1500 Mali is eclipsed by Songhai.

18th century The slave-raiding states of Ségou and Kaarta grow on either side of the Niger River. They are both conquered in the 1850s–60s by Tukulor Fulani.

1880–98 The French gradually penetrate the Mande areas, slowed by resistance by Mandinka warrior Samori Touré. He is defeated in 1898 after seven years of war.

1957 on West African countries gain their independence from foreign rule (mainly by Britain and France).

THE MANDE, OR MANDINKA, ARE ONE OF THE MOST DIFFICULT ETHNIC GROUPS TO DEFINE. THEIR CULTURE COVERS A LARGE AREA, EMBRACING MANY DIFFERENT WEST AFRICAN GROUPS WITH VARYING RELIGIOUS, LINGUISTIC, AND SOCIAL PRACTICES. TWO MAJOR GROUPS ARE THE BAMANA, WHO INHABIT THE GRASSLANDS AROUND BAMAKO, AND THE MALINKE, WHO LIVE IN MALI, GUINEA, AND CÔTE D'IVOIRE.

HISTORY

The Mande culture gave rise to two major West African states: the kingdom of Ghana, (5th–11th centuries) and the empire of Mali (13th–16th centuries). Ghana, with its capital at Kumbi Saleh (modern Mauritania), was well placed to profit from trans-Saharan trade. It was famed for its gold mines and traded in slaves, salt, copper, beads, and craftwork. The Mali empire was founded in the west of modern Mali but spread far wider. Its heartland of Mali lay on important trade routes, with access to gold mines and good farmland. Mali is remembered especially for its legendary founder Sundiata Keita and its powerful 14th-century rulers Mansa Musa and Abubakar II. Some rulers, including Mansa Musa, were so rich and so firmly in control of their dominions that they were able to undertake the long and arduous pilgrimage (hajj) to Mecca.

The rulers of Mali converted to Islam, although preexisting Mande religions continued to be practiced. Over time, Mali became a major Islamic center for the region, attracting scholars, architects, and students from all over the Muslim world.

The Mande were active in spreading Islam throughout the Sahel and into the forest zone. Mande traders are mentioned in

the history of the Hausa people, the *Kano Chronicle*, as bringing Islam to Nigeria in the 14th century. These missionary activities went hand in hand with commerce: the Mande traded gold, kola nuts, cloth, horses, metalwork, books, and salt widely in West Africa. Mande traders established themselves at the northern fringes of the forest, gaining access to the gold resources there.

The Mali empire declined from around 1500, but was succeeded by smaller city-states in the Mande heartland, such as the Bamana states of Kaarta and Ségou. Religious wars broke out between Islamized societies and those still practicing traditional religions. The Bamana put up especially strong resistance to the spread of Islam.

SOCIETY AND DAILY LIFE

Historically, Mande society was divided into distinct units. A group of Bamana villages formed a district controlled by a *fama* (leader) who came from a prominent family.

Bamana men perform a dance of homage to Ci wara, the mythical folk hero who is believed to have brought agriculture to the Mande. Because Ci wara was half-man, half-antelope, the elegant carved headdresses worn by the dancers represent male and female antelopes.

THE "LION KING" SUNDIATA KEITA

Sundiata—the "Lion of Mali"—was a boy-king who overcame great hardship to found the Empire of Mali in the 13th century. The epic tale of his struggle contains many timeless lessons, and formed the basis of the hugely successful Disney film *The Lion King* (1994). As a result, his story is now used by teachers in many classrooms in the United States to explore important questions, for example: What makes a hero?; How does Sundiata meet the challenges that face him?; and What qualities do Sundiata and the lion have in common?

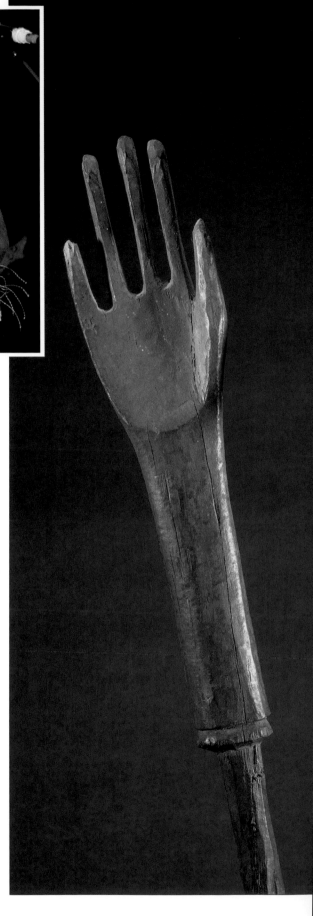

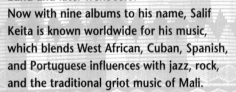

The musician Salif Keita (b.1949; the "Golden Voice of Africa") is a descendant of Sundiata Keita, founder of the Mali empire. This would have guaranteed him great status, except that Salif was born an albino. This is regarded as a sign of bad luck by the Mande people, and he was shunned by his family and community. Aged 18, he moved to Bamako and began his musical career by playing with bands in bars. He ultimately founded his own band and later went solo. Now with nine albums to his name, Salif Keita is known worldwide for his music, which blends West African, Cuban, Spanish, and Portuguese influences with jazz, rock, and the traditional griot music of Mali.

Salif Keita's fusion album Soro *(1987) brought Malian music to the world's attention and made the musician an international star.*

Bamana and Malinke families are also organized into *dyamu*. These were groups of people who shared the same name, male ancestors, and taboos—for instance a ban on eating animals that the *dyamu* considered sacred. Two famous Malinke *dyamu* are the Keita and Traoré families. Another Mande social group were the *nyamkalaw*, creative people born with the ability to master nature. The *nyamkalaw* comprised blacksmiths, leatherworkers, or bards (griots).

These categories still exist today, although urbanization and new earning opportunities are, like everywhere in the world, creating new social groups.

CULTURE AND RELIGION

The easiest definition of the Mande is through linguistic classifications; Mande are thus defined as people speaking one of the 71 Mande languages. The original heartland

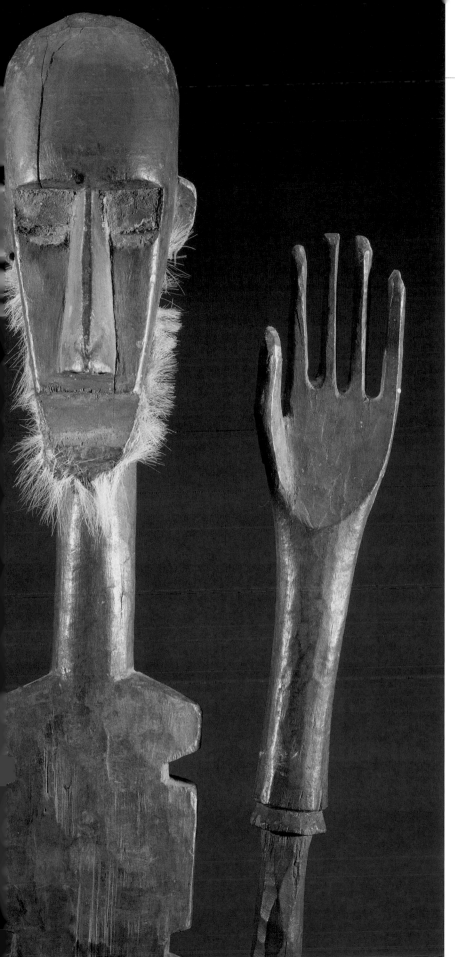

of the Mande-speaking area is the Upper Niger River, upstream of Bamako in modern Guinea and Mali. Mande ethnic groups can be broadly divided into the Sahel groups—the Bamana (or Bambara), Malinke, Dyula, Somono, Bozo, Khasonke, Marka, Soninke (or Serahuli)—and the forest groups: the Kuranko, Kono, Vai, and Susu-Yalunka.

Much Mande art is in the form of jewelry and carvings. Masks are especially important, and are used in community education. Tall Ci wara headdresses, which take the form of stylized antelope heads, are the best-known symbol of the Bamana. The Mande also produce beautifully woven fabrics and gold and silver necklaces, bracelets, armlets, and earrings.

Griots, who are specialist storytellers in the oral tradition, have long formed a central part of Mande culture. The most celebrated work of West African oral literature, the tale of Sundiata, founder of the Mali empire, comes from this culture.

SEE ALSO: *Fulani; Islam; Mossi; Music and musical instruments; Oral literature; Songhai.*

The Bamana Mande of Ségou in western Mali are known for their puppet shows involving marionettes such as this. Figures of people and animals are controlled by skilled puppeteers, and the plays often lampoon prominent people or neighboring peoples.

PUPPET THEATERS

Village puppet theater, which is widespread throughout West Africa, often forms an important part of a community's cultural life. Many puppets used by Sogolon Puppet Theatre Company (Mali) of the Bamana people are reputed to have been handed down through generations of the same family since the 19th century. Though puppetry remains principally a form of entertainment, it is also increasingly being used to teach vital lessons, for example in AIDS education campaigns in Togo, Ghana, and Mali.

MARRIAGE AND THE FAMILY

	Birth rate/ 1,000 population*	Infant mortality Deaths/1,000 births*	Fertility rate: Children born/woman (2005 est.)	HIV/AIDS in 2003 Living with (est.)	Deaths from HIV/ AIDS in 2003 (est.)
Benin	42	85	5.9	68,000	5,800
Côte d'Ivoire	36	91	4.9	570,000	47,000
Ghana	24	51	3.0	350,000	30,000
Mali	47	117	6.5	140,000	12,000
Niger	48	122	6.8	70,000	4,800
Nigeria	41	99	5.5	3.6 m	310,000
Senegal	35	56	4.8	44,000	3,500

* per annum (2005 estimate)

IN WEST AFRICA, FAMILY USUALLY MEANS THE EXTENDED FAMILY. THIS COMPRISES A HEAD OF HOUSEHOLD, HIS WIFE (OR WIVES), CHILDREN, AND ANY OTHER UNMARRIED OR ELDERLY RELATIVES. DESCENT IS TRACED THROUGH THE FATHER (PATRILINEAL) OR THE MOTHER (MATRILINEAL). YET SOME PEOPLES, SUCH AS THE FANTE OF SOUTHERN GHANA, TRACE THEIR DESCENT THROUGH BOTH.

Although polygamy is declining throughout West Africa, it is still practiced among many rural communities. The layout of this family compound of the Nankani people in northern Ghana reflects this custom, with low walls separating the huts of the chief's wives from one another.

Marriage is one the most rapidly evolving concepts in modern West African societies. In general, marriage is now increasingly regarded as an agreement between two individuals and their families, while practices such as polygamy (having more than one wife) are decreasing. That said, it is very hard to generalize, since marriage varies widely between particular groups, who attach very different cultural meanings to it.

FAMILY AND MARRIAGE PATTERNS

The family remains the primary unit around which West African societies are organized. The concept of the family is sacred, and certain actions, such as not helping a family member or disrespecting elderly relatives, are regarded as unacceptable. In the past, people attached great importance to the descent system. For example, among the matrilineal Asante a woman's brother, rather than her husband, was responsible for providing for her children.

Traditional attitudes toward marriage and gender roles were generally conservative. People strongly disapproved of sexual relations and pregnancies outside marriage, and took very seriously the separate obligations of husband and wife. Islam limited the number of wives a man could take to four. A man was expected to provide for his wife (or wives), while she was expected to take care of all the domestic arrangements and bear children. However, in many societies, a husband and wife were not obliged to live under the same roof. Divorce was common when one partner was thought not to be fulfilling his or her marital duties.

MARRIAGE, FAMILY AND SOCIAL CHANGE

In the late 20th and early 21st centuries the family and marriage have been heavily influenced by greater access to education, growing urbanization, and Christianity. The spread of Christianity means that

marriage is now increasingly seen as a religious rite. Many couples, especially in urban areas, now organize church weddings as well as performing traditional ceremonies. It has become more common for married couples not to live together and for the woman to be the head of the household, as many men travel to cities in search of work. The HIV/AIDS pandemic, although not as widespread as in southern Africa, has generated awareness campaigns promoting sexual abstinence before marriage, protection, and faithfulness to one partner.

SEE ALSO: African religions; Akan; Christianity; Islam.

Tuareg and Fulani health workers take part in a training program to raise awareness among these nomadic peoples of the dangers of HIV/AIDS. In countries such as Niger with low literacy rates, face-to-face sessions are a vital way of putting across information to combat the spread of the disease.

MASKS AND MASQUERADE

MASKS AND MASQUERADES HAVE LONG BEEN AN EXTREMELY IMPORTANT PART OF WEST AFRICAN CULTURES. AS WELL AS PLAYING A KEY ROLE IN FESTIVALS AND CEREMONIES, MASKS ARE ONE OF THE MOST STRIKING AFRICAN ART FORMS.

Two masks made by the Dan people of Liberia and Côte d'Ivoire. The masks embody a powerful spirit force known as gle, *which inhabits the region's forests and reveals itself to the carver in a dream. Each* gle *has its own personality, which the wearer takes on during the ritual. Poro masks were used to control the social and religious life of the Dan.*

HISTORY AND USES OF MASKS

The uses and forms of masks are prescribed by tradition. Masks are often associated with secret societies, initiation rites, and ceremonies. They are created for rituals that give center stage to spirits—the foundation of many African belief systems (see AFRICAN RELIGIONS). Thus, masked dancers may symbolize supernatural beings or ancestors in reenactments of scenes from the often complex mythology of a people.

In addition to this religious function, masks have many other social uses. They can, for example, signify discipline and control; in the masquerades of the Igbo, they are used to warn off uninitiated people such as women and children from witnessing the ceremony. Masks are worn to call for the gods' protection and help in ensuring, say, a good harvest or plentiful rainfall. They are also employed in funeral ceremonies (see box feature), fertility rites, or in curing sickness.

One of the most important uses of masks is in initiation ceremonies, also called rites of passage. These mark an important moment of change in a person's life—most

notably, the transition from childhood to adulthood. To prepare themselves, the adolescents withdraw from the community to an isolated place. There they are instructed in community laws and in their roles as adults. They are taught how to perform various rituals, and sometimes learn a secret language. Initiates also swear a solemn oath of secrecy, pledging not to reveal anything about their initiation. The ceremony customarily takes the form of a symbolic ritual of death and resurrection, signifying the "rebirth" of the initiate. The keynote of the whole process is to teach initiates about society. Accordingly, the

MASKS OF THE DAN

Among some of the Dan and Ngere groups of Liberia and Côte d'Ivoire, masks with distinct features represent ancestors, who act as intermediaries for sending petitions or offerings of respect to the gods. These ancestral emissaries use their spirit power to bring order and control to village life. The Dan are known for their semi-naturalistic, smoothly carved masks that represent materializations of spirits of the forest. Many of their masks are used to instruct initiates and relate to various social responsibilities, such as fighting fires and making peace.

Dancers from the Yacouba subgroup of the Dan people in Côte d'Ivoire wear masks at the annual Yam harvest festival.

masks used in these rites of passage personify the ancestors who were originally responsible for founding the tradition. These ancestor characters are powerful symbols of law and order. Among the Mende the Poro and Sande secret societies, for men and women respectively, use masquerades extensively in their initiation rites.

MASKS AS ART

An African mask is usually the work of highly skilled craftspeople, often being designed with graceful lines and displaying a highly polished surface. The *sowo* masks of the Sande masquerade of the Mende, for example, are intricately carved and polished heads depicting Mende ideals of feminine beauty. Also, beautifully stylized animal masks are common in West Africa.

Wood is the main material for African masks. In the tropical rainforests, many types of hardwood are available, for example, ebony, mahogany, and teak. Yet masks that are meant to be worn for lengthy dance rituals must be made from more lightweight woods; the Mossi of Burkina Faso use the wood of the ceiba tree for their often extremely tall and elaborately carved masks. Masks are rarely left as natural wood but are stained or colored with vegetable dyes. Certain colors have a special significance in particular rituals. In the 16th–18th centuries, in the Kingdom of Benin and among the Asante, ivory and even brass were also used to make masks for ceremonies performed by the ruling dynasty.

African masks vary to a great extent in their form, size, and shape. Some masks are an integral part of whole costumes or headdresses, while others are two-dimensional structures designed to cover only the face. Beads are also used quite widely as decorative items on masks.

European interest in West African masks increased greatly in the late 19th and early 20th centuries, as scholars began to study

THE DOGON KANAGA MASK

The Dogon of Mali have a highly distinctive wooden mask called the *kanaga*. Its symbolism is not easy to read. Some people believe that it represents a mythical bird of prey, the *konondo*, with the main body of the mask portraying the beak and the large crosslike structure above, with two lateral pieces of wood, symbolizing outstretched wings. Another explanation is that the tall superstructure is the "hand of God." The mask is used by members of the Awa society in ceremonies such as funeral rites; the dancers repeatedly dip their masks toward the ground to show the connection between earth and heaven. In these rituals, red, painted on the mask and also present in the dyed vegetable fiber skirts worn by the dancers, is a vibrant color intended to drive the soul of the dead person from his or her house and up to heaven. The *kanaga* is also worn in rites performed by hunters to protect themselves from the souls of the animal that they have killed.

them as cultural artifacts and collectors acquired them as works of art. Some Western modernist artists were strongly influenced by art forms from the West African region, foremost among which were masks.

MASQUERADES

Masquerades create a link between past and present, giving a sense of historic continuity that strengthens social bonds within the community. On these occasions, masks are worn or exhibited that represent dead hero chieftains, relatives, friends, or even foes. Gifts are sometimes made to the spirits embodied in the masks, while on other occasions dancers wearing stylized mourning masks perform the prescribed ceremony.

The preservation or disposal of masks is often decreed by tradition. Many masks—together with rules dictating their form and function—are passed down through clans, families, special societies, or from individual to individual. Often, the masks are spiritually "reactivated" and restored by being regularly repainted. In many instances, however, the mask is used only for one ceremony or occasion and is then discarded or destroyed, sometimes by burning.

SEE ALSO: *African religions; Akan; Contemporary art and photography; Dogon; Festival and ceremony; Igbo; Mande; Mende; Mossi; Sculpture.*

Members of the Dogon Awa society wearing kanaga *masks at the ceremony known as* daga, *which commemorates the anniversary of a death. The carving of such masks, which is entrusted to blacksmiths, only takes place after prayers have been offered to the tree spirit. After the* daga *ritual, the masks are discarded and left on the ground to rot away.*

MENDE

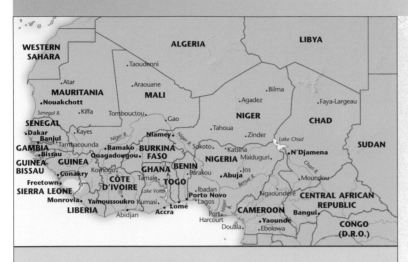

FACT FILE

Population	Sierra Leone 1,800,000; Liberia 19,700
Religion	Mende religion, Christianity, some Islam
Language	Mende, also known as Boumpe, Hulo, or Kossa, is a member of the Niger-Congo family.

TIMELINE

13th–15th century	Part of Mende territory is under the influence of the Empire of Mali.
1462–1700	Sporadic contact with European traders along the coast.
18th century	The slave trade, dominated by the British, displaces many Mende people.
19th century	After the abolition of slavery, Freetown, a British colony, becomes a center for former slaves. By 1850, over 100 ethnic groups live there in relative peace. In other areas, the century is one of warfare and disruption.
1880s–1890s	To fend off raiders, including the Islamic warlord Samori Touré, Mende groups form chiefdoms. Luawa, next to Liberia and Guinea, is one of the most powerful. The British take over in the 1890s.
1961	Sierra Leone becomes independent. The predominantly Mende Sierra Leone People's Party shares power with the All People's Congress.
1991–2000	Civil war spreading from Liberia and driven by competition for the control of Sierra Leone's diamond mines breaks out. Millions of dollars of diamonds are smuggled to finance rebels, and formal armed forces collapse as state and rebels alike rely on child militias. Some Sierra Leoneans, faced with the prospect of an imminent take-over of Freetown by rebels, demand to be recolonized by the British.
2002	President Ahmed Tejan Kabbah declares the civil war officially over. Sierra Leone slowly returns to stability.

THE MENDE LIVE IN WESTERN LIBERIA AND THE SOUTHERN HALF OF SIERRA LEONE, WHERE THEY FORM THE LARGEST SINGLE ETHNIC GROUP. THEY ARE WELL-KNOWN FOR THEIR "SECRET" SOCIETIES, TO WHICH MOST MENDE PEOPLE BELONG

HISTORY

Mende oral history tells of successive waves of migration that took place between around 200 and 1500 C.E. The fact that the Mende language is part of the much broader Mande language group (see MANDE) may support this idea. Certain cultural and physical characteristics also suggest that the Mende originated from several different groups of immigrants to the West African region.

In the early 19th century much of the Mende area witnessed great disruption and change. Immigration from the north and conflict in the south overwhelmed the region, and war became a near-constant feature of Mende life. To strengthen the defense of their communities, centralized chiefdoms were formed. Also, replacing the self-sufficient agricultural villages that had once been the norm, fortified towns were built, with narrow streets to prevent easy access by enemy forces.

SOCIETY AND DAILY LIFE

Most of the Mende live in rural areas, where they were historically rice farmers, and also grew yams and cassava as staple crops. Today, cocoa, ginger, groundnuts (peanuts), and palm oil are grown as cash crops.

Worn by a member of the exclusively female Sande society, the bondu *helmet mask and raffia costume represent a water spirit known as* sowo, *who escorts girls into initiation. The polished black mask, with rings on the neck, embodies Mende ideals of feminine beauty.*

Educational societies (known as Poro for men, and Sande for women) teach children about Mende law and crafts and help regulate society by laying down rules of behavior. They are commonly called "secret" societies because many aspects of their work are hidden from people who are uninitiated. The *bondu* or *sowo-wui* helmet mask, which is associated with the Sande society, is unique in being is the only known mask in West Africa to be used by women.

CULTURE AND RELIGION

The Mende excel in carving, singing, and storytelling. They also have a long tradition of mathematical calculation and an artistic writing system. In the religion of the Mende, which is still widely practiced, both evil and benevolent spirits make their presence felt in everyday life. Most art is associated with initiation and healing and includes wooden masks, twin figures, and medicine objects, carved and decorated so as to be pleasing to the spirits.

SEE ALSO: *African religions; Festival and ceremony; Mande; Masks and masquerade; Sculpture.*

MENDE NOMOLI

The ancestors of the Mende in what is now Sierra Leone were gifted in the art of carving in a soft stone known as soapstone, or steatite. Some of the most characteristic figures that they produced were *nomoli*. These small sculptures vary greatly in style, but usually depict a seated human figure with a bulbous head, prominent eyes, and a wide, flat nose. Their original purpose is unknown, although they may have represented clan or family ancestors. Mende farmers who unearth *nomoli* while plowing their fields place them in shrines, where they are used in ritual ceremonies to ensure that the rice crop will be protected.

FOR SOME 2,500 YEARS, METALS HAVE BEEN USED IN WEST AFRICA TO MAKE A WIDE RANGE OF CEREMONIAL AND DECORATIVE ARTIFACTS AND WEAPONS. THE REGION WAS ESPECIALLY FAMED FOR ITS BEAUTIFUL CAST METAL OBJECTS. MANY EXAMPLES OF THESE CAN BE SEEN IN MUSEUMS AROUND THE WORLD. TODAY, METALWORK REMAINS AN IMPORTANT PART OF WEST AFRICAN CRAFTS.

HISTORY

West Africans in what are now Nigeria and Niger were smelting iron by c.500 B.C.E. Iron took on a major role in making both tools and weapons; it is not known whether ironworking developed independently in West Africa or if it was introduced from across the Sahara. Yet the most highly prized metals in West Africa were copper and its alloys (bronze and brass). They were used to make elaborately decorated items of jewelry, as well as ritual objects. Although copper was mined in the Sahara and farther south and bronze was produced locally on a small scale, large quantities of metal only became available to the West African market through trans-Saharan trade and, later, by Europeans arriving off the Atlantic coast. The scale of this trade is indicated by the ton of copper and brass ingots that archaeologists discovered in a medieval camel caravan buried in sand and lost on its way across the Sahara. In the 16th century Europeans on the coast of Ghana could trade copper for gold on a weight-by-weight basis.

A Malian blacksmith working at his forge. Because blacksmiths were believed to be in league with supernatural forces in smelting and crafting metal, they were traditionally admired and feared.

The casting of gold, brass, or bronze has a long history in West Africa, and practitioners of this art reached a high level of skill. Famous examples of cast objects are the bronzes of Igbo-Ukwu from the ninth century (see box feature), and the brass plaques, figures, and busts created in the Kingdom of Benin from the 16th century on. These works were made using the lost-wax casting process. This technique involves making a clay mold around a model of the object to be cast. The inside of this mold is painted with wax to the desired thickness of the final, hollow metal artifact. The wax shell is then filled with a clay core, and iron pins are driven through the outer clay mold to hold the core in place. The mold is fired to melt out the wax shell, and then molten bronze is poured in. Once the metal has cooled, the inner core and outer cast are broken away to reveal the finished object.

Smaller, but no less exquisite, are the brass gold-weights made by the Asante in the 17th century. Cast in the form of animals (such as beetles, crocodiles, scorpions, fishes,

WEAPONS AND JEWELRY

In many African societies, iron is associated with destruction and authority. It was widely used to make weapons and ceremonial objects for rulers, including the curved *afena* knives of the Asante). Iron weapons made hunting and forest clearance easier, and likely facilitated the settlement of new areas. Among many West African peoples, blacksmiths are a special, separate caste regarded with both respect and fear by the rest of the community. The smelting of local iron ores, which had been practiced for at least 2,500 years, has died out since the 1950s with the import of cheap scrap metal from Europe.

Metal is also used for decorative items, such as jewelry. In most areas, gold is preferred but in and around the Sahara, the Tuareg and the Moors favor silver. These objects are sold purely by weight, even though some pieces involve intricate, incised designs that must have taken the craftsperson many hours to finish. This sector has adapted very quickly to tourist demand; cigarette cases, knives, and stylized animal figures are common sights in the modern West African marketplace.

SEE ALSO: *Akan; Igbo; Mande; Masks and masquerade; Moors; Tuareg; Yoruba.*

The Asante of Ghana are renowned for their goldsmithing. This exquisitely decorated pendant was worn as an insignia by an official at the court of the ruler, the asantehene.

and lions) or geometrical shapes, they were used by traders to measure gold dust. They have their origins in proverbs, maxims, sayings, legends and historical accounts.

The Yoruba are known for their iron healing staffs. These poles are dedicated to Osanyin, the deity (*orisha*) of medicine, and depict bird figures, which invoke the power of elderly women, who were supposed to take the form of birds and aid the healing process.

THE IGBO-UKWU BRONZES

Excavated in the late 1950s after a farmer had reported unearthing bronze finds near his home, the archaeological site at Igbo-Ukwu in southeastern Nigeria startled the world. No fewer than 721 objects were recovered, which radiocarbon dating determined as coming from the 9th and 10th centuries C.E. Extraordinary technical skills and artistry were involved in making these artifacts. They were cast as single pieces of bronze, onto which intricate details such as fine wire, insects, decorative twirls, or rosettes were then integrated. Some of these objects were found in a small shrine, while others had been placed at a burial site as grave goods. Igbo-Ukwu showed clearly that a rich and independent bronze-casting tradition had been developing from an early date in this part of West Africa.

MOORS

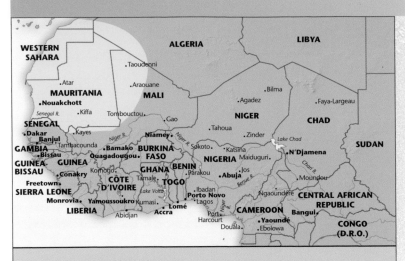

FACT FILE

Population	Mauritania 2,500,000; Mali 106,100
Religion	Islam
Language	Moors, both black and white, speak Hassaniya, which derives from the language spoken by the first Arab peoples who came to the region. It belongs to the Afro-Asiatic family, but is not mutually intelligible with the other 34 modern dialects of Arabic.

TIMELINE

pre-8th century	Archaeological remains and rock art in the Sahara Desert suggest that Mauritania was inhabited both by settled farmers and nomads from the north.
Late 8th century	Black populations convert to Islam and spread the faith to Senegal. The empire of Ghana, based in modern Mauritania, is a main channel of trans-Saharan trade.
11th–13th century	The Almoravids (a Berber dynasty from the Sahara) conquer the empire of Ghana. Mauritania is now fully integrated into the Muslim world.
15th–16th century	The arrival of Arab peoples, the Beni Hassan, modifies traditional Berber culture.
17th–18th centuries	Chinguetti, a key stop on the trans-Saharan trade route, becomes a major center of Islamic culture.
1900	The borders of modern Mauritania are determined by a treaty between Spain and France.
1960	Mauritania proclaims its independence.
1970s onward	Droughts increase migration to cities and stir ethnic tensions; Mauritania experiences many military coups.
1981	Mauritania officially abolishes slavery.
1991	U.N. brokers a ceasefire between Saharawis (Moorish Saharan nomads) of the Polisario Front and Morocco in 15-year war over control of the Western Sahara.

THE DESIGNATION *MOORS* (OR *MAURES*) WAS USED BROADLY IN THE PAST TO DESCRIBE THE INHABITANTS OF MOROCCO IN NORTH AFRICA, AND THE MUSLIM GROUPS THAT WERE DOMINANT IN SPAIN FROM THE EIGHTH CENTURY C.E. ONWARD. IN MODERN TIMES, IT DESCRIBES THE PREDOMINANT ETHNIC GROUP OF MAURITANIA ON THE NORTHWESTERN COAST OF AFRICA.

HISTORY

For thousands of years the territory of modern Mauritania has been inhabited by a variety of peoples. Among these were the so-called white Moors, nomadic peoples who looked to the north as their cultural homeland, as well as black Moors, settled farmers who lived in the south of the country. From the eighth century onward, the spread of Islam saw trade and contact across the Sahara increase dramatically. Although both black and white Moors adopted Islam, the degree of Arabic influence varied greatly from group to group. This is the root cause of the divisions that still exist in Mauritania, where white Moors, black Moors, and other ethnic groups conflict with one another over matters of language, land, and other issues. Slavery was officially abolished there in 1980 (for the third time), but it still exists in practice and its effects remain strongly felt.

SOCIETY AND DAILY LIFE

Broadly speaking, the white Moors, or Bidani, are nomadic cattle and camel herders of Berber–Arab origin. They account for some two-thirds of all Moors and play a dominant role in Mauritanian society. The black Moors—the Haratin or Sudani—are descended from the former black African captives of the Bidani, and make up the lower classes. Slavery is not just a historical condition for the Haratin; many remain in this position even today.

However, modern life is beginning to blur many of the clear distinctions that once existed between the two groups. Intermarriage has brought about some social mobility. Also, in recent years, drought has driven many formerly nomadic Moors to settle in urban areas, become seminomadic farmers, or take up work in the fishing industry. Many Moors still earn a living from trading, carried out today in local markets and towns. Others now work in the copper and iron mines in the northwest of the country.

In rural areas, nomadic Moors live in tents woven from wool. Men undertake herding and heavy agricultural work, while women make leather goods and weave cloth, including the fabric for tents. In cities, the well-off live in houses of adobe and brick, while the poor live in shanty towns made of sticks and cardboard.

CULTURE AND RELIGION

The most important celebration of the year for the Moors is the Duan festival, which takes place in September after the harvest has been gathered in. People clean their houses and cooking utensils thoroughly to welcome

THE TEA CEREMONY

Chinese tea, introduced to West Africa in the 15th century, now occupies a central place in the culture of the Moors (as well as other Saharan groups such as the Tuareg). The tea ceremony is a social occasion that gives its devotees a good opportunity to sit and talk for a long while. Tea is boiled on charcoals in a brightly colored metallic teapot with large amounts of sugar and served, frothy and very hot, in small glasses. These are emptied in one gulp and passed on for the next person to use. A complete tea ceremony consists of three successive brews, which are gradually weaker and sweeter.

the spirits of their ancestors. Horse racing, dramatic performances, feasts, and the beating of bronze drums also form part of the festivities.

Music and poetry are important in Moorish society and verses celebrating the legendary actions of chiefs and heroes are recited to the accompaniment of music played on traditional instruments.

SEE ALSO: Festival and ceremony; Islam; Metalwork; Music and musical instruments.

Desertification has been an increasing problem in Mauritania since the 1970s. It drove many Moors to abandon their nomadic cattle-herding lifestyle. Others, such as these herders, continue to live precariously on the edge of the Sahara.

MOSSI

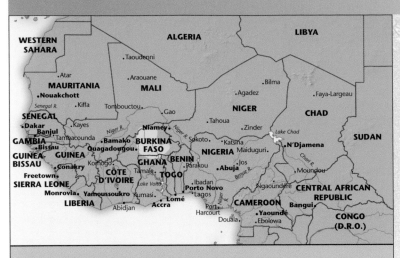

FACT FILE

Population	Mainly Burkina Faso 6.7 million
Religion	Mossi religion, Islam, Christianity. Religious tolerance is widespread and members of a same family often belong to different faiths
Language	The Mossi language, known as Mòoré, is part of the Niger-Congo language family.

TIMELINE

1400–1500	Mossi kingdom founded in Ouagadougou by Naba Oubri.
1500–1840	Further Mossi states emerge, all paying homage to the most powerful, Ouagadougou, and to its emperor, the moro naba ("great lord").
1800s	Different local powers and lineages compete for authority, fragmenting the Mossi empire.
1897	French colonial forces "divide and rule" the feuding Mossi states and take control of Ouagadougou.
1919–1950s	The Mossi are recruited to work on plantations and railroad building in Côte d'Ivoire; the former Mossi heartland is broken up for administrative and commercial convenience.
1960	The nation of Upper Volta is created, with Maurice Yameogo as president.
1966–early1980s	Yameogo is deposed by the military and imprisoned; more coups d'états follow in 1974, 1980, and 1982.
1983	Populist leader Captain Thomas Sankara seizes power and renames the country Burkina Faso (a Mòoré/Dioula name meaning "land of honorable people").
1987–92	Sankara is assassinated in coup led by his aide Blaise Compaoré; Compaoré retains power in 1992 elections.
2002	Tensions grow between Burkina Faso and Côte d'Ivoire.

THE MOSSI LIVE IN THE CENTER OF WEST AFRICA, IN THE MODERN STATE OF BURKINA FASO. FOR HUNDREDS OF YEARS THE MOSSI WERE NOTORIOUS FOR MOUNTING DEVASTATING CAVALRY ATTACKS ON THEIR NEIGHBORS

HISTORY

The first evidence of the Mossi is around the 14th century, when bands of horsemen from the south overran neighboring peoples such as Dogon, Lela, Nuna, and Kurumba. The invaders created a new state south of the bend of the Niger River, with themselves as chiefs and the conquered people as commoners. Over time, this state became a major political and military force in the region. In the mid-15th century the capital Ouagadougou was founded; it later became the permanent residence of the king, and is still the capital of Burkina Faso. Over the following centuries the Mossi successfully resisted invasion by the Muslim Fulani and Songhai.

In the early 19th century the Mossi empire broke down into internal warfare, which the French used to their advantage when they arrived on the scene in 1897. In the first decades of the 20th century, the Mossi were exploited by the new colonialists as a source of cheap labor. Independence was achieved in 1960 and the country was named Upper Volta. Its first president was a Mossi, Maurice Yameogo.

SOCIETY AND DAILY LIFE

The basic unit of Mossi society is the clan; several clans make up a district under the authority of the oldest member of the extended family (lineage), who is himself subject only to the king. Mossi society is patriarchal—that is, descent is traced through the father.

The Mossi are primarily farmers, growing millet, sorghum, corn, sesame, groundnuts (peanuts), and indigo plants. The last three are cash crops for export. In the past land was not owned by anyone, but rather used by the family, with elders allocating land to different households. In practice, this system still holds true today, although technically the government owns all the land.

CULTURE AND RELIGION

Most Mossi people are Muslim, though some still practice the Mossi religion, which is based on devotion to the ancestors. In the strict hierarchy of the Mossi kingdom artists were divided into guilds. Mossi art is still today used for both political and spiritual purposes. The ruling class (*nakomse*) uses masks and figures to stress its group identity and political authority; for example, during the annual celebration of the royal ancestors, figures of the dead kings are paraded. Masks are also used to invoke

A woman prepares a meal at a traditional Mossi village in Burkina Faso. The poor soil of the semiarid grasslands in the region and competition for land have meant that many Mossi have had to relocate their villages.

favorable weather and general well-being, and to avert disease and crop failure. On many occasions each year, especially during the long dry season from October to May, masks are put on display to honor the spirits of nature.

Ouagadougou is an important cultural center, which, among other events, hosts a two-yearly international film festival (Fespaco; see MOVIES).

SEE ALSO: Fulani; Masks and masquerade; Songhai.

MOSSI DOLLS

Many Mossi girls own *biiga*, dolls of wood and leather specially made for them by local carvers. They are stylized female figures, shaped like a tube, with a narrow semicircular head and, usually, no arms or legs. Although these dolls are toys, they also help prepare girls for future motherhood. Girls carry them around with them and care for them by rubbing them with butter and oils. The *biiga* remains important even beyond girlhood: when a woman marries, she takes her doll with her as a fertility symbol, to help her become pregnant.

WEST AFRICAN MOVIES AND MOVIEMAKERS

Title	Date	Director	Country
Xala	1975	Ousmane Sembène	Senegal
Ajani Ogun	1976	Ola Balogun	Nigeria
Love Brewed in the African Pot	1982	Kwaw Ansah	Ghana
Yeelen (Brightness)	1986	Souleymane Cissé	Mali
Yaaba (The Grandmother)	1989	Idrissa Ouédraogo	Burkina Faso
Hyenas	1992	Djibril Diop Mambety	Senegal
Buud Yam	1997	Gaston Kaboré	Burkina Faso
Moolade	2004	Ousmane Sembène	Senegal

WEST AFRICAN CINEMA IS A RELATIVELY RECENT PHENOMENON, ONLY DEVELOPING SINCE THE 1960S. THOUGH FACING MANY DIFFICULTIES OF FUNDING AND DISTRIBUTION, THE INDUSTRY NOW FLOURISHES, ESPECIALLY IN FRENCH-SPEAKING COUNTRIES AND IN GHANA AND NIGERIA.

BEGINNINGS

The first international success for West African cinema was the film *Borom Sarret* (Cart-Driver) directed by the Senegalese Marxist novelist Ousmane Sembène (b.1923) in 1963. His later film *Mandabi* (The Mandate) won a Silver Lion at the 1968 Venice Film Festival and inspired a whole

Posters advertise the products of the local movie industry in Nigeria. Movies are made in English and in Yoruba, the language of 19 million Nigerians.

People gathering for an open-air screening at the Pan-African Film Festival (Fespaco) in Ouagadougou, Burkina Faso, in 1997. This is Africa's most important movie event, where directors and others compete for a coveted Yenenga—the African equivalent of an Oscar.

generation of moviemakers. Many of them had been trained in the Soviet Union and knew the propaganda potential of movies.

EARLY THEMES

A major concern of African movies was, and still is, to challenge Western stereotypes of the continent and present African issues from an African perspective. Although African movies are made in many different countries, several common themes still emerge. These include the conflict between local values and those of the West, often expressed through the opposition between urban and rural lifestyles. Movies on this theme include *Kwami* by Togolese director Quenum Do-Kokou (1972) and *The Bronze Bracelet* (1974) by Tidiane Aw from Senegal. Other key themes are the alienation felt by Africans living overseas, the injustices of the colonial era, and exploitation by new elites. Early African movies were notable for their social and political comment, and often took their inspiration from African stories and legends. The 1970s witnessed an explosion of creativity in West African film industry.

THE OUGADOUGOU FILM FESTIVAL

Ougadougou, the capital of Burkina Faso, has become a center for the African film industry. Every two years, the city hosts the Pan-African Festival of Cinema (Fespaco). Full participation is limited to film-makers from Africa, but there is also a special category for films made by African-origin directors overseas, from the United States, Latin America, and the Caribbean. Several of the hits of the Ougadougou festival have gone on to win acclaim at other international events, such as Cannes. Examples include *Buud Yam* by Gaston Kaboré and *Yaaba* by Idrissa Ouédrago, both of whom are directors from Burkina Faso.

FRENCH-LANGUAGE CINEMA

The movie business in West Africa is much more advanced in Francophone (French-speaking) countries than in their English-speaking neighbors, and it is not unusual to see such movies broadcast on mainstream French television. One example of a highly successful movie from Francophone West Africa is *Yeelen* (Brightness) by Souleymane Cissé, which explores the conflict between a father and his son as they try to preserve the memory of precolonial Africa. This movie won a major prize at the 1987 Cannes Film Festival. Niger, Cameroon, and Burkina Faso are also developing movie industries. Burkina Faso produced Gaston Kaboré's prizewinning *Buud Yam*, about a hero's search for his parents and his own identity.

GHANA AND NIGERIA

In English-speaking West Africa, only in Ghana and Nigeria has moviemaking developed beyond the production of government-sponsored documentaries. Well-known directors include King Ampaw and Kwaw Ansah, whose *Love Brewed in the African Pot* combines music, wedding ceremonies, and sports events to help tell the story, a technique that has met with significant commercial success in many African countries. A distinctive feature of Nigerian cinema is the production of movies in the Yoruba language as well as in English, a reflection of the country's very large Yoruba population. The themes treated are similar to those in other West African movies, but Yoruba cinema also draws upon a centuries-old tradition of theater. For example, the film *Ajani Ogun* starred a top theater actor, Ade Love.

Abuja in central Nigeria hosts an international film festival, a four-day event for local and international moviemakers.

SEE ALSO: English-language literature; French-language literature; Oral literature.

MAJOR STYLES AND KEY PERFORMERS

Style	Artist	Country
Afro-Beat	Fela Anikulapo-Kuti	Nigeria
Fuji	Ayinla Kollington	Nigeria
Highlife	Alex Konadu	Ghana
Highlife	Rex Lawson	Nigeria
Juju	King Sunny Ade	Nigeria
Manding	Toumani Diabaté	Mali
Mbalax	Youssou N'Dour	Senegal
Afro-Cuban Dance	Orchestra Baobab	Senegal

THE MUSIC OF WEST AFRICA IS RICH AND VARIED, AND HAS ABSORBED MANY DIFFERENT INFLUENCES OVER THE CENTURIES. WITH THE RISE OF INTEREST IN "WORLD MUSIC" SINCE THE 1980S, THE WORK OF MANY OUTSTANDING WEST AFRICAN PERFORMERS HAS BECOME MORE WIDELY KNOWN.

West Africa has enormously diverse musical traditions. One of the most widespread forms is Manding music, which is played by the Mande people of Mali and many other countries of the region, and uses the kora as one of its key instruments. This is a 21-stringed harp made using leather strings attached to a rosewood pole, which is inserted through a large, decorated half-gourd or calabash. In the top of the body of the instrument is a large sound hole that can also serve as a collection box for donations from the audience. The kora is often accompanied by the *balo*, a rosewood xylophone, and by two kinds of lute, one with five strings, the other with three or four strings.

Lutes and harps of various kinds are also used extensively in the music of Burkina Faso, Mauritania, Gambia, and Senegal. Drums are also important, ranging in size from the large *tbol* (kettledrum) of Mauritania, through the *kalungu* talking drum of Nigeria, to the small hourglass-shaped *tama* of the Wolof people of Senegal. Farther south, thumb pianos (mbira or *sanza*), xylophones (*balafon*), and lutes (*ngoni*) are common in Sierra Leone, and drums among the Ewe and Asante of Ghana. Some instruments are particularly distinctive, for example the water flutes and baobab tree fruit trumpet (*xokudu*) of Togo's Kabyé people.

A group of traditional musicians performing at the International Roots Festival in The Gambia uses a variety of West African instruments, including the kora and the balafon.

MUSICAL CASTES

In many areas there exists a professional caste of musicians. Among the Mande only certain families—such as the Konté, Kouyaté, and Diabaté—are entitled to bear the title *jali*, or hereditary musician, and the playing of most instruments, as well as the recital of epic poems and family histories, was once reserved for them. Comparable groups include the *igaouen* of Mauritania and the three classes of professional musicians found among the Fulani. Fulani *wammbaabe* and *maabube* are still primarily court musicians, who have the task of praising chiefs and other wealthy patrons, mostly using the *hoddu*, a three-stringed lute. *Awlube* musicians are the third group and are less closely associated with courts and leaders. They play a much wider range of instruments, but especially drums. Percussive instruments such as rattles and gourds are also common among professional troupes of Fulani entertainers.

The world-famous Senegalese singer Youssou N'Dour (b. 1959) was born into a Wolof musical griot caste, traditionally praise singers and storytellers. With his band 'Super Etoile de Dakar,' Youssou N'Dour is a leading performer of *mbalax*, a popular musical form characterized by complex percussion rhythms and influenced by Caribbean (especially Cuban) music.

HIGHLIFE, JUJU, AND FUJI

Highlife, juju, and *fuji* are three of the most successful forms of modern popular music to come out of West Africa. Highlife originated in the 1920s through the fusion of European influences like hymns and brass bands with traditional percussion and melodies. It caught on quickly in Ghana and Sierra Leone, where it was introduced by Liberian sailors. The name itself comes from the 'highlife' of dressing up and going out to dance in the city. Several different styles exist, the two main ones in Ghana being

guitar bands (for dancing) and concert party bands (which combine music with dance, stories, and comedy). E. T. Mensah, Nana Kwame Ampadu's African Brothers International Band, Daniel Amponsah, and Alex Konadu are among the leading Ghanaian performers, with Bobby Benson and Rex Lawson the main figures in Nigeria.

Juju (from the Yoruba *jo jo*, meaning "dance") has gained ground in Nigeria at the expense of highlife. Originating around Lagos in the 1930s, it thrived during and after the Biafran War of 1967–70, with I. K. Dairo, Ebenezer Obey, and King Sunny Ade among its leading artists. Native languages, mostly Yoruba, dominate in this style of music, as they do in the third of Nigeria's main modern music forms, *fuji*, which also has roots in traditional Yoruba music. A fourth form, Afro-Beat, uses pidgin English and is especially associated with the political protest music of Malian Fela Anikulapo-Kuti.

The Rail Band was formed in 1970, with sponsorship from Mali's railroad administration and the Ministry of Information. The group quickly became very popular, and is still performing today.

SEE ALSO: *Ewe; Festival and ceremony; Fulani; Mande; Wolof; Yoruba.*

THE BUFFET BAR, MALI

Manding music has had a major influence on the development of popular music in post-independence West Africa, and the reciting of traditional epic songs by *jalis* or griots still continues today. As musicians sought to rediscover their precolonial roots in the 1960s the Buffet Hôtel de la Gare in Mali's capital, Bamako, became a major venue. Its resident Rail Band launched the careers of many famous vocalists, including Salif Keita (b.1949; see MANDE) and Mory Kanté (b.1950). A distinctive feature of the Rail Band was its mix of Islamic vocal styles with traditional Mande rhythms played on modern electric instruments. Of those musicians to emerge from this background, Keita in particular has gone on to great international success, with albums including *Soro*, *Ko-Yan*, and *Safari Ambience*.

EXAMPLES OF ORAL LITERATURE

The **Epic of Sundiata** tells the struggle of the boy-king who overcomes adversity to found the ancient Mali empire. It is available in an English translation by D. T. Niane: *Sundiata: An Epic of Old Mali* (1970).

The work of **Hampâté Ba** (1901–91), a Fulani traditionalist from Bandiagara, Mali. Ba warns of the loss of home-grown knowledge and culture through Western influence. His books include *Amkoullel l'enfant peul* (Amkoullel The Fulani Child) and *Oui mon commandant* (Yes, Sir).

The writings of **Massa Makan Diabaté** (1938–88), descendant of a long line of griots. Among the ten books he wrote, the most well-known are his trilogy *Le Lieutenant, Le Coiffeur,* and *Le Boucher de Kouta* (The Lieutenant, The Hairdesser, and The Butcher of Kouta) which won the 1987 Grand Prix International de la Fondation Léopold Senghor.

THE MALIAN POET HAMPÂTÉ BA'S OBSERVATION "WHEN AN OLD PERSON DIES, IT'S LIKE A LIBRARY GOING UP IN FLAMES" UNDERLINES HOW VITAL THE ORAL TRADITION IS IN PRESERVING FOLK MEMORY. STORYTELLING BOTH TEACHES AND ENTERTAINS, AND IS STILL THRIVING IN MODERN WEST AFRICA.

Before the arrival of Islam with its tradition of scholarly writing (around 1000 C.E.), and the later influence of Christian missionaries and colonial officers, writing things down was not a common practice in West Africa. Instead, stories, family trees, and historical accounts were passed down by word of mouth from teller to teller. These narrators were sometimes part of a special group within the community (for example, the *jali* or griots of the Mande), and were usually old people with great wisdom.

Oral literature combines education and entertainment, and so plays an important part in moral and civic education. A published version of the Epic of Sundiata (see MANDE), probably the most famous piece of oral literature from West Africa, opens with the line "I teach kings the history of their ancestors so that the lives of the

A Hausa griot delivers a praise song. Across West Africa, griots act as keepers of the history of a people. They are not only musically gifted, but have exceptional memories, and can recite long histories and genealogies by heart.

GRIOTS

Griots are a special caste of learned storytellers, musicians, entertainers, and historians whom a lineage or a group entrust with preserving and retelling its past. They are found throughout the Sahel region of West Africa from Senegal in the west to Niger in the east, although the areas inhabited by the Mande are their heartland. Today, they have become known far beyond the borders of West Africa through the work of singers who come from a griot background, such as Salif Keita (see MANDE, MUSIC AND MUSICAL INSTRUMENTS) and Youssou N'Dour (see WOLOF). Yet some commentators believe that the tradition has been compromised by contact with the outside world: Malian griot novelist Massa Makan Diabaté has written: "The griots died with the arrival of the whites."

ancients might serve them as an example, for the world is old, but the future springs from the past."

Oral literature can also function as history. The *Kano Chronicle* and the *Diwan Salatin Bornu* of Kanem Borno, which were only written down in the 19th century, trace the family trees (genealogies) of their peoples—the Hausa and Kanuri respectively—back to the 10th or 11th centuries C.E. Similarly, the epic poems known as the *Dausi* are sung and narrated by the Soninke people, a subgroup of the Mande living in present-day Senegal. In ancient times, the Soninke were citizens of the empire of Ghana, which was at its height in around 800 C.E., and the Dausi recount the part-mythical, part-factual history of the city of Wagadu. The poems relate how this magnificent city disappeared four times—the last time forever—because of human weaknesses such as vanity, greed, deception, and disunity. The seminomadic

Fulani celebrate their history in epic poems called the Baudi. These poems arose from the warlike past of this people; when Fulani noblemen went on campaign they took with them singers (*mabo*), who also served as their shield bearers. The singers recorded the heroic exploits of their masters in the *baudi*.

The defining characteristic of oral literature is the fact that it does not rely on written manuscripts (making the concept of "oral literature" rather a contradiction in terms). Oral literature is transmitted through performances, in which particular themes are stressed depending on the audience, and familiar phrases and gestures are employed. All this helps root knowledge in its social context, and emphasizes strongly that the performers and audience have a common heritage.

SEE ALSO: African-language literature; Festival and ceremony; Fulani; Hausa; Kanuri; Mande; Music and musical instruments; Wolof.

Kandia Kouyate (right) is a jalimusolu, *or female* jali, *from Mali. She was schooled in the performance style of the Manding* griot, *and has become famed across West Africa for the power of her voice.*

SCULPTURE

WEST AFRICAN SCULPTURE COMES IN MANY SHAPES AND FORMS, AND EMPLOYS A WIDE RANGE OF MATERIALS, INCLUDING WOOD, CLAY, STONE, AND IVORY. FROM THE WOODEN STOOLS, CLAD IN PRECIOUS METALS, THAT SERVE AS ROYAL REGALIA AMONG THE ASANTE TO THE BRASS BUSTS, PLAQUES, AND FIGURES MADE IN THE KINGDOM OF BENIN, SCULPTURE FROM WEST AFRICA IS ADMIRED WORLDWIDE.

Most African sculpture, and this region is no exception, is not made for purely artistic ends. Instead, statues, masks, carvings, and ceramics all have a powerful symbolic content, communicating the values of the societies that make them. Yet, for all their social function, they also reveal a highly developed sense of appropriate form and beauty—which art historians call "esthetics."

CLAY SCULPTURE

One of the oldest and most widespread sculptural traditions in West Africa is the use of clay. Clay sculpture is often called terracotta (literally "fired earth") and is produced by the same method used to make pottery. Women play a key role in pottery making across West Africa, so it is likely that many, maybe even most, of the clay sculptures of the past were also made by female artists.

The oldest examples come from the Nok Culture of eastern Nigeria. Dated to around 500 B.C.E., the Nok terracottas include human heads and statues, as well as animal figures. Other, more recent, cultures have also used clay to produce sculptures in widely varying styles. For example, the Koma of northern Ghana made relatively crudely modeled human busts, while those

Small soapstone figures (left) were created by coastal peoples around present-day Sierra Leone. Called nomoli by the Mende, they were placed in shrines and brought offerings of thanks for good harvests.

PLUNDERING THE PAST IN MALI

European and American demand for African sculpture and other art forms has greatly increased since the late 20th century. This demand has stimulated an industry making mostly low-quality items for the tourist trade, and a black market in the illegal export of valuable original artifacts. Museums and galleries often still collude in this latter trade, even though they know that the items concerned have been stolen. Looting of artworks has been especially problematic in Mali, where ancient towns and cemeteries, such as those as at Djenné and Gao, have been systematically plundered for metalwork and terracotta statues. The terracotta pieces are often elaborately modelled, with people shown wearing rich jewelry and clothing, though animals are also represented. At least some may have illustrated spirits or ancestors, but their production ceased some centuries ago, probably because Islam forbids representative art.

made for the royal courts of Ife and Benin in Nigeria are highly naturalistic representations of prominent men and women that were originally kept in shrines. Mali's Middle Niger Valley is another area where clay sculpture once thrived. Elsewhere in West Africa, the practice of sculpting in clay survived until recent times, especially in funerary (burial) art.

Some modern artists Nigeria's Oshogbo School (see CONTEMPORARY ART AND PHOTOGRAPHY) specialize in cement sculpture.

SOAPSTONE AND STONE

Stone has been relatively little used in West African sculpture, but some examples are known. In around 1200–1500 C.E., for instance, the carving of soapstone figures was common among the Yoruba in the Esie area of southwestern Nigeria. Some centuries ago, almost all of these figures were destroyed, apparently deliberately, making any clear interpretation of them difficult. However, like the better-known clay and metal sculptures from nearby Ife, it is

This terracotta rider and horse was found in a burial mound in the Middle Niger region of Mali, around Djenné and Mopti. Made in the 13th or 14th century, it reveals the potter's skill in crafting the intricate necklace the man is wearing and the horse's elaborate bridle.

thought that they were made for rulers and other high-ranking people. Farther to the east, the Cross River area is home to large decorated stone monoliths that may have been made to commemorate dead ancestors. Sierra Leone and neighboring parts of Liberia and Guinea form the other main area of stone sculpture, again using soapstone. Mostly of human figures, these carvings are now often worshiped in shrines as spirits or ancestors by the Mende and Kissi peoples.

SCULPTURE IN METAL

Across West Africa copper and copper alloys (bronze and brass) have long been valued as precious metals that embody a spiritual power. These metals were widely used to create free-standing sculptures, primarily of human figures, for members of the elite; perhaps the best known of these are the brass heads of kings and queens (*onis*) made at Ife from around 1150 onward. These stunning naturalistic sculptures testify to the great technical skill of their makers in mastering the lost-wax process (see METALWORKING) for casting metal. Other superb examples of precolonial Nigerian craftsmanship are human figures from Tada and Tsoedde, and the many cast brass figures and plaques from the kingdom of Benin, which was at its height in the 15th and 16th centuries. The fineness of the work involved strongly indicates that they were produced by specialist craftsmen.

WOOD CARVINGS

Plentifully available both in this region and elsewhere in sub-Saharan Africa, wood was by far the most common medium for sculpture. However, because it is vulnerable to fire, damp, and insect attack, relatively

The Dogon of Mali traditionally used forked wooden posts to support the beams of their village toguna, *or council meeting houses. These posts were carved with ancestor figures in an abstract style.*

few examples survive from before the colonial era. West African wood carvings range from the funerary art of Nigeria's Oron and Kalabari peoples to masks and free-standing figures. Unlike clay sculptures, wood carvings are mainly made by men. The carvings had, and still have, a wide range of social uses. Among the Kundu of Cameroon, for example, they are used by the Musongo society to administer oaths to establish a person's guilt or innocence. In Côte d'Ivoire, the Baule people and others create male and female figures to represent spirits, while the Senufo use wooden sculptures in the initiation rites of the Poro secret society. For many peoples, especially the Asante, wooden stools are a mark of kingship and the 'enstoolment' of a king or chief is a solemn occasion equivalent to a coronation in Europe. Doors are another form of wooden sculpture; those made for granaries by the Dogon are particularly elaborate, reaching high prices on the international art market.

SEE ALSO: *Akan; Dogon; Funeral and reliquary art; Masks and masquerade; Mende.*

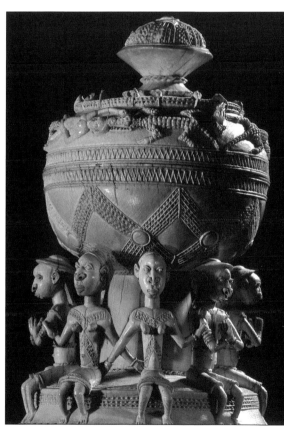

Commissioned by Portuguese sailors who visited the Guinea coast, Sapi ivory carvings were the first goods from Africa made especially for export. This exquisite saltcellar has four male and four female figures in European dress seated around its base.

AFRO-PORTUGUESE IVORIES

African peoples, who had long been in contact with other parts of the world, became adept at tailoring craft objects from their own culture to foreign tastes, so as to exploit trading opportunities. The ivory carvings made by the Sapi people from the coast of Sierra Leone in the 15th and 16th centuries are a fine example of this enterprise. Fusing African and European stylistic elements, the Sapi designed saltcellars, spoons, and other objects expressly for export to Europe, where they were prized by aristocratic collectors.

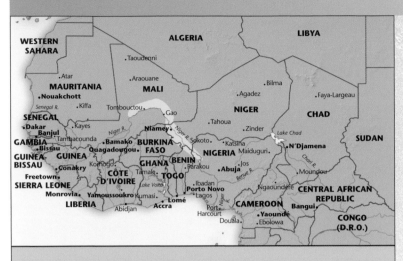

FACT FILE

Population	Niger 2,570,000; Mali 738,000; Burkina Faso 125,000; Nigeria 90,000; Benin 30,000
Religion	Islam, Songhai religion, Christianity
Language	Songhai, which is part of the Nilo-Saharan family, includes eight more or less mutually intelligible dialects, of which Zarma has the most speakers. There is also a mixed Berber-Songhai language, Tagdal, spoken by about 27,000 people in Niger.

TIMELINE

7th–11th centuries	The Za dynasty rules the Songhai empire, first from Kukiya then from Gao, both on the Niger River bend in eastern Mali; Islam is adopted c.1000 through contact with Arabic cultures across the Sahara.
1290s–1340s	The Empire of Mali absorbs Songhai, but the Sonni dynasty slowly free Songhai from Malian rule.
1464–92	Reign of Sonni leader Ali Ber; he drives the Tuareg from Timbuktu and greatly extends Songhai's influence.
1493–1528	Songhai empire reaches its height under Askia Muhammad I, covering much of present-day Mali and Niger.
1591	A Moroccan army defeats Songhai.
17th century	Written accounts of Songhai history appear, composed in Timbuktu and Djenné.
1618–1787	Moroccan puppet state rules over Timbuktu and surrounding area until overrun by the Tuareg.
1898	French colonial forces complete their conquest of former Songhai lands, which are incorporated in the territory known as French Sudan.
1988	Tombouctou is listed as a UNESCO World Heritage site.
2004	The Tomb of Askia Muhammad in Gao is listed for preservation as a UNESCO World Heritage site.

THE SONGHAI, A SETTLED PEOPLE WHO LIVE ALONG THE NIGER RIVER IN MALI AND NIGER, TRACE THEIR HISTORY BACK TO THE GREAT SONGHAI EMPIRE. FROM ITS CAPITAL GAO, THIS STATE RULED OVER MUCH OF THE WEST AFRICAN SAHEL—THE SOUTHERN FRINGE OF THE SAHARA—IN THE 15TH AND 16TH CENTURIES.

HISTORY

The origins of the Songhai are obscure. Oral history tells of specialist groups—fishers, hunters, and farmers—originally living along the Niger River. About 1,000 years ago they came together to form the state of Songhai. Under three dynasties, Songhai grew into one of the most important trading empires of West Africa. Its rise to prominence began in the reign of Ali Ber (r.1464–92) who crushed the power of the Mali empire, and beat off attacks by the Mossi, Dogon, and Fulani.

Islam gradually gained ground in Songhai, becoming the state religion under the Askia dynasty, which ruled from 1493 onward. In the 15th and 16th centuries the city of Tombouctou (Timbuktu) became a major center of Muslim learning and culture. There was a privileged caste of craftsmen, and slave labor played an important role in agriculture.

In the late 16th century Songhai, already weakened by civil war and drought, was invaded by Moroccan armies intent on controlling trans-Saharan trade. Yet their dominance was short-

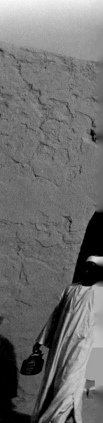

THE TOMB OF ASKIA MUHAMMAD

In around 1495 Askia Muhammad I, who was a devout Muslim, made Islam the official religion of Songhai. To commemorate this event and to emphasize the might of his empire, the ruler ordered the construction of an imposing tomb for himself in the city of Gao. Standing 50 feet (15 m) high, the pyramid-shaped tomb uses the traditional mud-building techniques of the Western Sahel. It is surrounded by two flat-roofed mosques, a cemetery, and an open-air assembly ground. It was listed as a UNESCO World Heritage site in 2004. Thousands of visitors come to this site each year.

lived, with the Segu empire becoming the main regional power by the mid-17th century. Timbuktu was overrun successively by the Bambara, Fulani, and Tuareg, and finally the French, who captured the city in 1893. For most Songhai people, however, life continued unchanged on the banks of the Niger River.

SOCIETY AND DAILY LIFE

Songhai villages along the Niger River contain rice paddies and market gardens, where vegetables and fruit are grown. Villages farther from the river are surrounded by bush and cultivated fields, with groundnuts (peanuts), millet, cowpeas,

When Mansa Musa, ruler of the Mali empire, liberated Timbuktu (Tombouctou) from the Tuareg in 1330, he celebrated his victory by having the Djinguereber Mosque built. Islam continued its spread throughout the Songhai region over the next 150 years.

and cassava the usual crops. Some livestock is also kept. Villages are arranged according to kinship groups, and all the men have a common male ancestor. Following Islamic custom, a man can take up to four wives.

CULTURE AND RELIGION

Though the Songhai are predominantly Muslim, spirit possession and the veneration of ancestors are still strong elements of their faith. Important festivals include Genji bi hori, at which offerings are made to the spirits that control disease, and Yenaandi, which asks for rainfall. Songhai culture is best known for its epic poems, which are still today recounted by the bards and chroniclers known as griots.

SEE ALSO: *African religions; Architecture; Fulani; Mande; Mossi; Oral literature; Tuareg.*

TEXTILES

WEST AFRICA IS JUSTLY FAMOUS FOR THE BEAUTY AND VITALITY OF ITS TEXTILES. A VARIETY OF RAW MATERIALS ARE USED: LOCALLY GROWN COTTON, CAMEL AND SHEEP WOOL, RAFFIA PALM, JUTE, FLAX, ACRYLICS, AND SILK. THE REGION IS ESPECIALLY RICH IN ITS DIVERSE WEAVING TRADITIONS, AND A THRIVING INTERNET MARKET HAS DEVELOPED FOR ITS FABRICS.

Textile production has a long history in West Africa: 14th-century travelers reported that Kanem-Borno was exporting saffron-dyed cloth. By the 19th century, the Hausa lands were making large quantities of cloth. Textiles were also widely used as a currency, for example among the Wolof. Textile manufacture in West Africa today embraces both a modern, high-volume industry and craft weaving.

WAX PRINTS

Foremost among the colorful modern textiles that one can see daily on any West African city street are "wax prints," so called

A man strip-weaving at a narrow double-heddle loom. Heddles are parts of the loom that pick up and pull down the warp of the cloth—the threads running lengthwise—to let the weft (the crosswise fibers) through. Strip-weaving is common throughout West Africa.

because they are made using stencils and wax. Patterns are printed in wax on strips of cloth, which are then dipped in dye. With the wax preventing the dye from soaking into the fabric in the areas where it had been applied, a basic pattern is created. Then the fabric is put through machines that partially break off the wax, resulting in an arbitrary pattern, with no two lengths of the cloth quite alike. The fabric is then pattern-printed with up to three more colors. This form of textile manufacture has global origins: it was inspired by Indonesian batik fabric-printing techniques, and was developed in Europe specifically for export to Africa. By the 1950s, many countries in West Africa had started their own production of such materials; Senegalese and Nigerian "wax," for example, are highly regarded today. However, the most sought-after of these wax prints, used in West African traditional dress, do not actually come from Africa but from the Netherlands. Wax prints are made industrially, but there is also a lively manual cloth production sector, usually by men on hand looms.

FABRICS AND STATUS

Particular styles of weaving are specific to cultures or ethnic groups, to different genders or different age sets. Elaborate textiles can signify greater wealth or social standing, while special clothes are reserved for important social occasions such as weddings or funerals. Some of the most famous examples of traditional fabrics and attire that are made manually are Asante kente from Ghana, Bambara *bogolan* from Mali, Hausa boubous from Niger and Nigeria, and Fulani wedding blankets from throughout the Sahel.

Kente cloth, originally worn only by high-ranking figures among the Asante people of Ghana, is used today not only to decorate the Ghanaian parliament and courts, but also throughout the African diaspora

Kente being made in Bonwire, Ghana, the historic royal center for production of this cloth. The overall look of the finished piece is carefully planned, with design elements on each strip lining up in a checkerboard pattern.

worldwide as a popular symbol of Pan-African identity. A folk tale traces its origin to two friends from Bonwire who came across a spider weaving its web and were so impressed that they decided to imitate it, and

THE IWELEN GOWN

The archaeological site of Iwelen is located in a valley in the Saharan mountains of Aïr, in Niger. It includes former dwellings, rock art, and funerary monuments, and was occupied for several thousand years. Of the many graves that have been excavated, one was especially striking—a burial mound about 7.5 feet (2.3 m) in diameter on a gravel base. In this the skeleton of a woman was found, wrapped in a leather shroud still fastened by wooden pins, wearing a green and red gown and a shawl probably influenced by North African weaving methods. She was buried over a thousand years ago, and her gown is among the oldest known textiles in West Africa.

so created the first kente. The first kente cloths were all cotton, but from the 18th century onward Asante weavers began to incorporate imported Dutch silk. Today, rayon (artificial silk) is widely used. Kente cloth is woven in narrow strips and sewn together, with distinct patterns and designs commemorating historical events and figures, household objects, or proverbs. It is often predominantly gold in color. The *keta* cloth of the Ewe people is also strip-woven like kente and uses contrasting colors between the warp and the weft of the cloth.

BOGOLAN, BOUBOUS, AND BLANKETS

Another African cloth tradition known around the world is *bogolan*, known as *bokolanfini* (literally "mud cloth") in the language of its makers, the Bambara, who are a subgroup of the Mande people. Plain white cotton cloth woven by men in narrow strips are sewn up into a wider cloth and then dyed, usually by women, using pounded leaves and various mixtures of mud and clay: specialists have closely guarded recipes to give the best results. Craftswomen then decorate the cloth using spatulas of various widths to draw designs with a mud solution. When this is dry, the pattern is repainted using a soap made of ash and vegetable oil and then covered with more mud. After the cloth has been allowed to dry completely, the mud and wax is scraped off, taking the dye beneath off as well and exposing the pattern. High quality *bogolan* can take several weeks of painstaking work before the whole cloth is covered. Typically, designs are geometric and abstract, but items made for the tourist trade can be more representational, showing, say, scenes from village life.

Boubous are gowns with long sleeves or a shirt that slips over the head. The most impressive men's garments, which consist of a gown worn over a shirt and trousers, require up to 30 feet (9m) of cloth. They are

ALPHADI—AN AFRICAN FASHION GURU

Nigerian fashion designer Alphadi (b.1957; real name Seidnaly Sidhamed) has won acclaim throughout West Africa and Europe as the face of modern African haute couture. His designs, which incorporate Songhai, Fulani, Hausa, and Tuareg influences, are produced in his Niamey fashion house, employing 65 people. Alphadi's goal is to establish African fashion as a source of jobs and human development, and as a way of projecting a more positive image of Africa than is often reported in the media. In 1998 he launched the International Festival of African Fashion (FIMA), which brings together African and Western fashion designers.

fashions. The Hausa of Nigeria and Niger are famous for their boubous, which are called *riguna*. The shape of the garment does not vary greatly, although some are more 'flowing' than others. On the other hand, the quality of the cloth—damask is the most highly rated—and the detail of the embroidery immediately mark out a man of power and wealth. The designs embroidered on the garments, for example the amulet motif, are thought to have Islamic origins. Many of these designs are now machine-stitched but their patterns remain unchanged. Two classic ones are "two knives" and "eight knives," named for the sharply pointed shapes worked into the design.

Fulani wedding blankets (*arkila* or *kaasa*) are woven for engaged couples. It is said that spiritual energy is woven into the pattern, and that the weaver must never stop working partway through the design. The couple must bring the weaver food and kola nuts to keep him awake until it is finished. Once married, they keep the blanket in their house, and it is brought out any time they have an argument, to remind them of the love that originally brought them together.

SEE ALSO: *Akan; Ewe; Fulani, Hausa; Islam; Leatherwork; Mande.*

Using mud fermented in a jar for a year, a Bambara textile worker from Mali prepares bogolan *cloth. This craft was originally reserved for women, but men are now becoming more involved.*

richly embroidered at the cuffs, around the collar, and on the hem of the garment. Today, although the embroidery is often done with sewing machines, it is still impressively intricate.

The origin of these garments is not known, but may be associated with the spread of Islam. They have gradually gained prominence throughout West Africa over the last 200 years, demonstrating the dynamism of West African textile industries and

ANCIENT SPINDLE WHORLS

Spindle whorls are used in the craft of spinning fibers by hand into threads for weaving. They are pierced objects, typically made in the shape of a flattened spool, that fit onto the end of a thin rod and, when made to spin, gather fibers onto the rod. This produces a thread that can then be used for weaving cloth. In West Africa, spindle whorls are often made of clay, which is then incised with beautiful, intricate designs. Several of these artifacts have been found on archaeological sites covering the past 1,000 years. They are also much in demand in the tourist trade as decorative items and antiques.

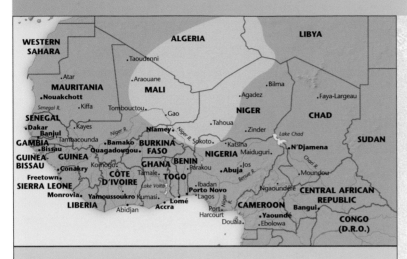

FACT FILE

Population	Not easily assessed, but significant populations include: Algeria 25,000; Burkina Faso 25,000; Libya 17,000; Mali 440,000; Niger 720,000
Religion	Islam, with strong preexisting beliefs.
Language	All Tuareg speak *Tamasheq*, a Berber language. Four dialects exist, all mutually comprehensible. Many people, especially women, can also write using the *tifnagh* alphabet. Arabic script is also widely used.

TIMELINE

3000 B.C.E.	Berber ancestors of Tuareg settle on North African coast.
300 C.E.	Camels in widespread use in the Sahara.
700 onward	Islam introduced into the Sahara.
1043–1147	Almoravid fundamentalist movement uses Tuareg and other Berbers to help spread and strengthen Islam.
1431	Tuareg overrun Timbuktu as Mali empire crumbles.
1500	Songhai empire assimilates many Tuareg groups.
1591	Songhai conquered by Morocco.
1600–1900	Tuareg play a central role in trans-Saharan trade.
1902–18	French conquer the Tuareg in a series of military campaigns.
1960	Mali and Niger win independence (plus Algeria 1962).
1963	Tuareg revolt in Mali harshly put down.
1968–74	Major droughts in the Sahara and Sahel force many Tuareg to move and seek new land and/or food relief.
1982–85	Terrible droughts recur, further damaging the Tuareg.
1990	Tuareg rebellions break out in Mali and Niger.
1996–97	Tuareg sign peace accords with Mali and Niger.

BERBER ANCESTORS OF THE TUAREG INHABITED THE WESTERN AND CENTRAL SAHARA FROM AROUND 3000 B.C.E. AS WELL AS REARING LIVESTOCK AND TRADING ACROSS THE SAHARA, IN THE PAST THE TUAREG HAD A FIERCE REPUTATION FOR RAIDING AND WARFARE. IN MODERN TIMES, THE TUAREG HAVE COME INTO CONFLICT WITH THE STATES THAT RULE OVER THEIR TERRITORY.

HISTORY

More properly known as *Kel Tamasheq* (meaning "those whose speak *Tamasheq*," a Berber language), the Tuareg are found across the western and central Sahara. Their direct ancestors lived there since at least the early centuries C.E., when the camel was introduced to the region. However, they probably descend from still earlier Berber-speaking pastoralists, while genetic data also suggest ancient connections with the Beja of Northeast Africa. Tuareg expansion across the areas they now inhabit has been a long process, perhaps linked to the ancient Garamantian state (c.500 B.C.E.–500 C.E.) and later encouraged by the Almoravid Islamic movement and the growth of the Songhai empire. However, some areas have only been occupied since around 1800. When the French colonized the region, they only managed to suppress the Tuareg with great difficulty. Since the nations of the Sahel won their independence in the early 1960s, the Tuareg have found themselves spread between several states. Repression and discrimination (including denial of famine relief), forced resettlement and general poverty, aggravated by sustained periods of drought, have fueled Tuareg separatist movements and wars in Mali and Niger.

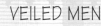

SOCIETY AND DAILY LIFE

Tuareg society was based on a caste system, with the highest caste, the *immaggeren*, forming a military class that exploited both pastoralists (*imrad*) and slaves (*iklan*). The *iklan* were largely sub-Saharan black Africans and provided the labor force for farming the Saharan oases, an occupation that was held in contempt by the higher castes. Other subgroups were the *inadan* (blacksmiths) and *inesleman* (priests), both of which would travel and attach themselves to *immaggeren* camps. Politically, the *immaggeren* and *imrad* were part of a group of tribes that formed larger confederations, each headed by a chief, or *amenokal*. Kinship ties, both matrilineal (through the mother) and patrilineal (through the father), were used to settle control of livestock and labor.

VEILED MEN

Unlike other Muslims, among the Tuareg it is men, not women, who wear a veil. This garment is known as the *tagelmust*. Men take the veil on becoming adults; it is thought to ward off evil spirits, though it also has the practical purpose of protecting them against wind and sand. The *tagelmust* is also a mark of a person's respect for others, especially elders. A man keeps his mouth covered at all times in the presence of others, and in the company of senior people will allow only his eyes to be seen. Tuareg veils, turbans, and robes are usually made of cloth dyed dark blue with indigo. This plant dye, which often stains the wearer's skin, has earned the Tuareg the name "The Blue Men of the Sahara" in popular accounts of their culture.

A veiled Tuareg camel rider. While many Tuareg remain nomadic, drought and warfare have forced others to settle and become dependent on tourism, aid, or farming.

Daily life in the past centered around the care of livestock, particularly camels, goats, and sheep. Because of the limited grazing available in the Sahara, people and animals moved between one pasture and another, but within well-defined territories. Cereals were obtained from slave farmers, in trade, or were gathered wild.

CULTURE AND RELIGION

Art and music both play an important part in Tuareg life. Jewelry (made in silver, which is seen as the purest metal) and leatherwork are well-known crafts. Tuareg forms of the violin and drum are the most common instruments played at parties and festivals, such as camel races. The musical group Tinariwen have achieved considerable international success by fusing traditional Tuareg music with electric guitars.

The Tuareg are Sunni Muslims, who combine Islam with several preexisting practices, among them a belief in spirits that have the power to possess people, especially women. Other spirits are thought to live in fire and their power can be accessed by the *inadan* blacksmiths. The Tuareg pitch their tents in a particular direction in order to gain protection against evil spirits. The wearing of protective amulets bearing verses from the Quran is also widespread.

SEE ALSO: Fulani; Hausa; Islam; Metalwork; Music and musical instruments; Songhai.

WOLOF

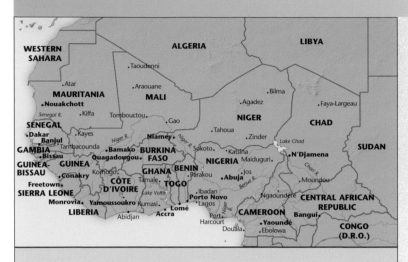

FACT FILE

Population	Senegal 4,000,000; Gambia 255,000
Religion	Islam
Language	Wolof is part of the Niger-Congo language family. In Senegal, especially in urban areas, Wolof is fast becoming the main national language, with members of other linguistic groups learning it as a second language. Senegalese Wolof is mutually intelligible with that of Gambia but with significant differences.

TIMELINE

11th–15th centuries	Wolof ancestors migrate to the coast after the empire of Ghana collapses, and convert to Islam.
14th century	The Wolof are unified in the Wolof empire.
1455	Alvise Ca da Mosto, a Venetian explorer and trader, describes the Wolof kingdom of Kayor (part of the fragmented Wolof empire).
1500–1815	Wolof traders deal in slaves through the fort at Gorée.
1850–64	The Tukulor caliphate of al-Hajj Umar briefly becomes the dominant power in the region.
1850s–1900	The French annex Wolof territories and make Dakar the gateway to their colony of French West Africa. Inspired by the example of the Tukulor leader al-Hajj Umar, the Wolof kings resist the French for over 30 years.
1960	Senegal becomes independent from France.
1987	Gorée Island listed as a UNESCO World Heritage site. Its architecture is characterized by the contrast between the grim slave-quarters and the elegant houses of the slave traders.
1980s–2004	Southern province of Casamance, protesting Wolof dominance, rebels against the Senegalese government.

MOST WOLOF PEOPLE LIVE IN SENEGAL, WITH SMALLER NUMBERS IN THE GAMBIA AND MAURITANIA. ALTHOUGH THERE ARE SOME REGIONAL DIFFERENCES BETWEEN THESE GROUPS, THE WOLOF ARE UNITED BY A COMMON LANGUAGE, A STRONG ETHNIC IDENTITY, THEIR TRADITIONAL SOCIAL SYSTEM, AND THEIR FIRM COMMITMENT TO ISLAM.

HISTORY

Wolof history dates back to around the beginning of the 13th century, when various small groups unified to form the Wolof empire, a loose political federation with its center in northwestern Senegal. This state later fragmented under pressure from political intrigue, rebellion, and warfare.

In the 15th century Europeans established a fort on Gorée Island (near the modern Senegalese capital, Dakar), which became the largest slave-trading center on the African coast. The Wolof were involved in capturing and selling slaves, which brought them into contact with many different peoples. In the 1850s, the French attempted to conquer the Wolof kingdoms, which sparked decades of war. A major factor in the powerful resistance that the Wolof put up against the colonial invaders was the unifying force of their Islamic faith.

SOCIETY AND DAILY LIFE

The basic subsistence crop is millet, while the main cash crop is groundnuts (peanuts). Cassava is also grown, both as a cash crop and for food. Chickens, goats, and sheep are kept for meat; rice and dried or smoked fish is purchased from other groups.

Groups known as *ker*, who occupy their own separate areas, are the basic social unit

in Wolof villages. Each *ker* is based around an extended family, which may include a man, his brothers, their wives, and their children. The senior male of the dominant family unit leads the *ker* in allocating fields, settling disputes, and representing the group in village affairs. *Kers* belong to wider lineages and often pay a portion of their income to the lineage head in return for use of the land—a practice the Senegalese government is trying to abolish.

Migration from rural to urban areas is common. Although most Wolof are still rural villagers, they also make up a significant element in many of Senegal's urban centers.

In the past, Wolof society was marked by its strong caste system, with a person's status determined by their birth. Categories in this hierarchy include noblemen, warriors, farmers, traders, craftsmen, bards (griots), and—formerly—slaves. This system is still a key aspect of social life in the country, and even continues to play a role in the cities.

CULTURE AND RELIGION

Islam is the dominant religion of the Wolof people, and major festivals include Ramadan and Tabaski (a Wolof word now used throughout Muslim West Africa for the Eid ul-Adha festival). Wolof are active in Muslim brotherhoods (*tariqa*); men normally follow their fathers, while women join their husband's brotherhood when they get married. The Mourides brotherhood, which follows a strict Islamic code of hard work

Gorée Island was established in the late 1400s as a slave trading post. A total of 2 million people are estimated to have passed through here. The Wolof were involved in capturing and selling slaves to the Europeans.

and clean living, is very influential. Its center is at Touba in western Senegal.

Many Wolof art forms incorporate beautiful inscriptions, including copies of passages of the Quran enclosed in intricate boxes or leather pouches, and depictions of respected Islamic teachers.

SEE ALSO: *Fulani; Hausa; Islam; Music and musical instruments.*

THE SET SETAAL MOVEMENT

In Wolof, Set Setaal means "be clean and clean up." In 1990 a group of young people in Dakar got together under this banner to try to regenerate their urban environment. They took the name of their movement from the title of an album by their hero, the Wolof singer Youssou N'Dour. They cleaned up illegal garbage dumps, restored water supplies, and painted powerful political protest murals. These wall paintings showed scenes from Senegalese history (including the slave trade at Gorée), advice on combating AIDS, diarrhea, dysentery, and malaria, as well as portraits of famous African, American, and European figures. The movement was soon taken up by the authorities, which saw it as a good opportunity for social education.

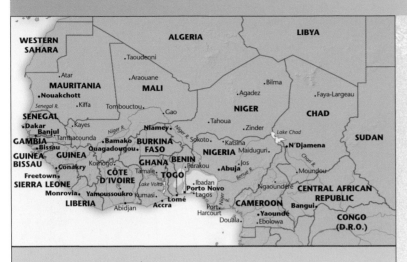

FACT FILE

Population	Nigeria 27,000,000; Benin 465,000
Religion	Yoruba religion, Christianity
Language	Yoruba is part of the Niger-Congo language family. Up to 2.5 million people speak Yoruba as a second language.

TIMELINE

6th century	Ile-Ife is occupied by this time.
late 15th century	Oyo becomes a small kingdom, aided by cavalry imported from the Sahel and Portuguese firearms.
c.1450–1650	Edo Kingdom of Benin, legendarily founded by a Yoruba prince, rises; it is renowned for its sculpture.
17th–18th century	Oyo eclipses both Ife and Benin and reaches its peak, largely through slave trade profits.
1807–17	Abolition of slavery and loss of European market reduces the price of slaves, making them affordable to local buyers. Large numbers of Hausa slaves in Yoruba lands revolt; civil war breaks out in Oyo.
1830s	The Fulani Sokoto Caliphate conquers Oyo.
1830–80	Formerly enslaved Yoruba return home from Brazil and Sierra Leone.
19th century	Hundreds of thousands of war refugees migrate to the south of the Yoruba area; new towns founded, e.g. Ibadan and Abeokuta (center of Yoruba Christianity).
1888–1901	British colonize the Yoruba lands.
1960	Nigeria attains independence.
2002	Nigeria calls for the return of Yoruba and other indigenous works of art from the British Museum.
2005	Oshun Sacred Forest, Oshogbo is listed as a UNESCO World Heritage site.

THE YORUBA LIVE PRINCIPALLY IN SOUTHERN NIGERIA AND BENIN. THEIR SACRED CENTER IS ILE-IFE, WHERE YORUBA MYTHS STATE THAT THE WORLD BEGAN. THE YORUBA ARE KNOWN FOR THEIR ARTISTIC EXPERTISE, ORAL LITERATURE, LARGE PANTHEON OF GODS, AND URBAN LIFESTYLE. IN PAST TIMES, MILLIONS OF YORUBA WERE SHIPPED TO THE AMERICAS AS SLAVES

HISTORY

Yoruba society is thought to have developed when village compounds gradually amalgamated into territorial city-states. The most important of these was Ile-Ife (now a part of Ife, a city in southwestern Nigeria). Ile-Ife is known to have been occupied since at least the sixth century, and was a major settlement between the ninth and 12th centuries. From around 1250, the center of power shifted to the cities of Oyo in the grasslands to the northwest.

After Europeans arrived in West Africa, slavery began to play a key role in the economic and political development of the Yoruba lands. Wars were both a cause and a consequence of slave raiding. A succession of civil wars finally came to an end when British forces annexed the Yoruba territories in the late 19th century. Many works of art from this region were plundered and taken to museums in Britain.

SOCIETY AND DAILY LIFE

Historically, the Yoruba were farmers, growing yams and oil palm. Later they cultivated crops that were introduced to West Africa by Europeans from the Americas, such as cocoa, corn, cassava, and groundnuts (peanuts).

A 19th-century wooden mask made for the masquerade of the Gelede society. This ceremony is held annually to appease and entertain the aje, which are destructive, malevolent female spirits.

Yoruba society was not governed by a single, central authority but instead was based around several towns, each of which presided over by a leader (*oba*) assisted by a council of chiefs. These towns had been in existence centuries before Europeans arrived. Craftspeople and traders operated there, and the concentration of wealth allowed a complex market economy to develop. The arts also flourished in these urban centers.

The decentralized nature of Yoruba society made for strong regional allegiances and unity, but also left it highly vulnerable to the spread of colonialism.

CULTURE AND RELIGION

The Yoruba have several hundred deities (*orisha*), most of whom are actively worshipped. Their supreme god is Olorun, or Olodumare. Major festivals honoring the gods take place throughout the year and are attended both by followers of the Yoruba religion and by Christians. One of the most famous events is the Oshun Festival (see FESTIVAL AND CEREMONY) held in Oshogbo every August. In addition, yearly sacrifices and rituals known as Egungun masquerades remember deceased members of a lineage. Homage is paid at ancestors' graves during these ceremonies.

The arts of the Yoruba are as diverse as their gods. Objects are placed on shrines, and masks are used at funerals. Yoruba art of the past is known worldwide through beautifully crafted terracotta and brass heads and figures from Ile-Ife. These were made between the 12th and 19th centuries, and relate to the *obas*.

SEE ALSO: *Festival and ceremony; Hausa; Igbo; Masks and masquerade; Metalwork; Sculpture.*

GELEDE MASKS

The Gelede ceremony, which takes place every year between March and May in the southwestern corner of Yoruba territory, commemorates the special power of women, who can be both givers and takers of life—mothers or witches. The celebration of Gelede is meant to protect people from the power of witches through the use of magic, percussion, sculpture, dress and dance, and masks, of which there are thousands of different kinds. They are worn exclusively by men, but portray a wide range of male and female characters.

Any of the words printed in SMALL CAPITAL LETTERS can be looked up in this glossary.

adinkra Religious signs used by the Asante people of Ghana.

adobe Dried clay or mud, widely used as a building material throughout Africa.

afena A curved hunting knife used by the Asante of Ghana.

age-grades The different social level in certain societies. Each person is part of an "age-set" (a group of similar-aged peers) who move up as they grow older through the various age-grades, gaining in status.

agriculturalist A settled (sedentary) farmer who makes his or her living by cultivating crops.

Allah The Islamic name for God. Like Christianity and Judaism, Islam is a monotheistic religion (that is, it has only one God).

arkila A blanket woven especially for a newly married couple among the Fulani. It is seen as symbolic of the love between them, and is a highly treasured possession.

asantehene The Asante king.

balafon A percussion instrument, similar to the xylophone, used widely in West Africa. It is usually made of wooden keys attached to a CALABASH.

Bidani Historically, the ruling caste (also known as "White Moors") in traditional Mauritanian society.

bogolan The characteristic dyed fabric (also called mud cloth) made by the Bambara people. Mud is used to mask off different areas of the cloth while it is being dyed.

boubou A loose-fitting gown widely worn by West African men; they are often richly embroidered, and worn over trousers of the same cloth and pattern.

calabash A type of gourd. Its hollowed-out shell is used for a variety of purposes in West Africa, from containers to musical instruments such as the KORA.

clan A social group made up of several extended families or LINEAGES. Clan members often trace their descent from a common ancestor.

Dausi A cycle of spoken epic poems telling the history of the Soninke people, a subgroup of the Mande.

Gelede Annual ceremonies, held by the Yoruba people, to celebrate the power of women and appease local witches.

gri-gri A good-luck charm used in West Africa. Fishers, for example, place them on their boats to ensure favorable weather and a good catch.

griot A storyteller, singer, and musician in West Africa. These bards form a special caste (social group), and are responsible for chronicling a community's oral history.

groundnut An alternative name for the peanut, a staple food and major cash crop for many peoples of sub-Saharan Africa.

hajj The annual pilgrimage to the holy city of Mecca in Saudi Arabia to pray at Islam's holiest shrine, the Kaaba, and undertake other religious duties. It is one of the "Five Pillars" (essential holy duties) of Islam, and so long as a person has the means to do so, she or he is expected to undertake the journey at least once during her or his lifetime.

hale Educational societies of the Mende, which teach initiates about the laws and customs of the people. The most important are the Poro society for men and the Sande society for women.

Haratin Historically, the lower caste (also known as "Black Moors") in Mauritanian society. They are descendants of the former captives of the ruling BIDANI.

Ikeji The most important festival among the Igbo people of Nigeria. It celebrates the new yam harvest, and takes place annually between August and October.

Immaggeren The highest rank in the caste system of the Tuareg NOMADS of the Sahara. Formerly a military class, it ruled over all other castes, including the Imrad (PASTORALISTS), Iklan (slaves), Inadan (blacksmiths), and Inesleman (priests).

jali A term used by the Mande for a GRIOT. It is reserved for certain families who have belonged to the musician caste for centuries. A female jali is called a jalimusolu.

jihad (Arabic "struggle") In Islam, the struggle a person undertakes to submit to Allah. It may involve armed struggle, and so is often translated as "holy war." Some Muslim authorities see it as a sixth "pillar," or basic duty of Islam.

kankouran A shaman (spiritual guide to the community) among the Mande people.

kente A fabric woven in narrow strips by the Asante, and regarded as the national dress of Ghana. It is decorated with complex, symbolic designs, some incorporating ADINKRA.

ker In Wolof society, an extended family that forms the basic social unit of a village.

keta Strip-woven cloth produced by Ewe weavers. It uses complex patterns and contrasting colors for the WARP and WEFT, and is similar to the KENTE of the Asante.

kora A 21-stringed harp made from a gourd (CALABASH) and a rosewood pole, and widely played in West Africa.

lineage An extended family group that shares a common ancestor. If the society traces its origins to a male ancestor and descent is traced from father to son, the lineage is termed patrilineal. If the ancestor is female and descent is traced from mother to daughter, the lineage is matrilineal.

lost-wax casting A metal-casting technique used by West African craftspeople. It involves making a wax model of the object to be cast and encasing it in a clay mold. When the mold is heated, the wax melts and molten metal is then poured into the cavity through a hole in the mold.

makuba A building material, made from clay and oil of the locust-bean tree, used by the Hausa to make distinctive plaster designs on the outside of houses.

marabout An Islamic holy man or mystic, especially among the Moors of Mauritania.

masquerade A festival in which masks and costumes are worn. Many African cultures have elaborate masquerades marking important RITES OF PASSAGE such as initiation.

mbalax A form of popular music with complex percussion rhythms, played in West Africa (especially Senegal). Influenced by Cuban and Caribbean music, one of its most well-known performers is the Wolof singer Youssou N'Dour.

Morocco leather The high-quality, soft red leather produced in the Hausa regions of northern Nigeria and Niger. Its misleading name comes from the fact that Western traders in the Middle Ages purchased the leather from Morocco.

mosque An Islamic place of worship.

nakomse Historically, the ruling class among the Mossi people of Burkina Faso.

negritude (French: "blackness") A literary movement founded in the 1930s by West African and Caribbean expatriates in France. Its aims were to celebrate African culture and oppose colonial rule.

nomad (adj: nomadic) A person who follows a wandering lifestyle, usually living either by herding livestock or trading. The movements of nomads, such as the Bedouin or Tuareg of the Sahara, are determined by the need to find new grazing pastures, or by trade demands.

oba A king of the Yoruba people.

oni The title of a ruler—king or queen—of the former Ife kingdom of the Yoruba in Nigeria.

orisha (or orisa) In the Yoruba religion, one of a PANTHEON of several hundred deities.

pantheon A group of gods (such as the gods of ancient Greece, or the Yoruba ORISHA), each of whom has control over a different aspect of life.

pastoralist A person who lives by herding livestock such as cattle or sheep and generally pursues a nomadic or seminomadic lifestyle.

polygyny The practice of marrying more than one wife.

Quran The holy book of the Islamic faith. It consists of verses (*surahs*) and is regarded by Muslims as a direct transcription of the Word of ALLAH recited to Muhammad by the angel Jibril (Gabriel).

Ramadan The ninth month of the Islamic calendar, held holy by Muslims as the month during which ALLAH called Muhammad to be His Prophet. Muslims fast between sunrise and sunset during Ramadan. The end of the month is marked by a major celebration known as Eid ul-Fitr.

reliquary (adj. and noun) A container used to hold the remains of a person, or a term to describe such a vessel.

rite of passage A ceremony, such as initiation into adulthood or marriage, that marks the passage of a person from one stage of life to another.

Sahel A semidesert region south of the Sahara separating it from the savanna (grasslands) farther south. Vegetation is sparse and there are frequent droughts.

scarification The practice of adorning the body or face by making shallow cuts in the skin, which heal to form permanent scars. Scarification is associated in many cultures with initiation rituals marking a person's transition from childhood to adulthood. Scarification is infrequently practiced today.

shantytown An area of impermanent housing, usually made from scrap materials, on the outskirts of large cities where poor migrants to urban areas live. Shantytowns often lack running water, drainage, and other basic amenities.

Sharia (Arabic: "divine law") Islamic law. Sharia is based both on the edicts established by the prophet Muhammad in the QURAN and on the practices that Muhammad observed during his lifetime, which later Islamic scholars formulated as guidelines regulating the lives of Muslims.

shifting cultivation A farming method (once termed "slash-and-burn" agriculture) that involves clearing an area of forest for temporary crop growing. After harvesting the crop, the farmers move on to a new location.

subsistence farming A type of agriculture in which all the crops grown are eaten by the farmer and his family, leaving nothing to sell for profit ("cash crops") at market.

Sudanic style A style of building, influenced by the Muslim cultures of North Africa, which became widespread in the Sahel from the 13th century onward. It is characterized by the use of adobe walls and wooden beams (TORON).

Tabaski The Wolof term, used throughout West Africa, for the Islamic festival of Eid ul-Adha, the commemoration of Abraham's willingness to sacrifice his son Isaac.

taboo A restriction or prohibition, established by convention in a culture, which prevents a person from acting in ways regarded as inappropriate. Many taboos relate to tasks that must not be undertaken by one sex or the other, food that must not be eaten, or certain forms of clothing that may not be worn.

tagelmust A veil worn by Tuareg men, both as a protection against desert sand and as a way of obeying the Islamic regulation of hijab, the injunction to dress modestly.

tariqa Muslim brotherhoods that became influential in West Africa from the end of the 18th century. The Muridis brotherhood among the Wolof of Senegal is a powerful modern religious and social institution.

toron Wooden beams protruding from the sides of adobe buildings in the SUDANIC STYLE. They strengthen the structure and provide scaffolding for repairing the adobe walls.

urbanization The process by which a rural area becomes more built-up and industrialized.

vodu (plural: "vodun") A spirit or deity in the Fon religion. The plural form "vodun" is also generally used to denote the Fon religion. It is thought to be the origin of the word *voodoo*, the religion that descendants of Fon slaves developed on the island of Haiti in the West Indies.

warp The lengthwise threads in a woven cloth.

wattle-and-daub A building technique that uses clay or adobe plastered on a latticework made of sticks.

weft In a woven cloth, the threads that run across the WARP.

General books:

Beckwith, C., and Fisher, A. *African Ceremonies* (Harry N. Abrams, Inc., New York, NY, 2002).

Hynson, C. *Exploration of Africa* (Barrons Juveniles, Hauppauge, NY, 1998).

Mitchell, P. J. *African Connections: Archaeological Perspectives on Africa and the Wider World* (AltaMira Press, Walnut Creek, CA, 2005).

Morris, P., Barrett, A., Murray, A., and Smits van Oyen, M. *Wild Africa* (BBC, London, UK, 2001).

Murray, J. *Africa: Cultural Atlas for Young People* (Facts On File, New York, NY, 2003).

Philips, T. (ed.) *Africa: The Art of a Continent* (Prestel, Munich, Germany, 1995).

Rasmussen, R. K. *Modern African Political Leaders* (Facts On File, New York, NY, 1998).

Sheehan, S. *Great African Kingdoms* (Raintree/Steck-Vaughn, Austin, TX, 1998).

Stuart, C., and Stuart, T. *Africa—A Natural History* (Swan Hill Press, Shrewsbury, UK, 1995).

Temko, F. *Traditional Crafts from Africa* (Lerner Publishing, Minneapolis, MN, 1996).

The Diagram Group *Encyclopedia of African Peoples* (Facts On File, New York, NY, 2000).

The Diagram Group *Encyclopedia of African Nations and Civilizations* (Facts On File, New York, NY, 2003).

Thomas, V. M. *Lest We Forget: The Passage from Africa to Slavery and Emancipation* (Crown Publishers, New York, NY, 1997).

Books specific to this volume:

Beckwith, C., and van Offalen, M. *Nomads of Niger* (Collins, London, UK, 1984).

Davidson, B. *West Africa Before the Colonial Era: A History to 1850* (Longmans, London, UK, 1998).

Giles, B. *Myths of West Africa* (Raintree/Steck-Vaughn, Austin, TX, 2002).

Giles, B. *Nigeria (Nations of the World)* (Raintree/Steck-Vaughn, Austin, TX, 2004).

Glasse, C., and Smith, H. (eds.) *New Encylopedia of Islam* (AltaMira Press, Walnut Creek, CA, 2003).

Keenan, J. *Sahara Man: Travelling with the Tuareg* (John Murray, London, UK, 2003).

Quigley, M. *Ancient West African Kingdoms: Ghana, Mali, and Songhai* (Heinemann, Oxford, UK, 2002).

The Diagram Group *History of West Africa* (Facts On File, New York, NY, 2003).

Thompson, C. *The Empire of Mali* (Franklin Watts, Danbury, CT, 1998).

Useful Web sites:

www.coraconnection.com
Information on West African music.

www.ecowas.int
Web site of the Economic Community of West African States.

www.fespaco.bf/index_en.html
Web site of the Ougadougou-based FESPACO film festival.

www.ghanaweb.com/GhanaHomePage
Online resources for Ghana.

www.h-net.org/~wafrica
Discussion forum on West African culture and history.

nigeriaworld.com
Covers many aspects of contemporary Nigeria.

www.svn.net/rkovach/oware
Detailed guide to one of West Africa's most popular games.

webworld.unesco.org/goree/en/index.shtml
Virtual visit to Gorée island, a major center of the former transatlantic slave trade.

PICTURE CREDITS

OVER NIGHT BOOK

This book must be returned before the first class on the following school day.
